D1133544

Roberto G. Salvadori

THE JEWS OF FLORENCE

From the Origins of the Community
up to the Present

Translated by Ann Curiel

Giuntina

CONTENTS

PREFACE

This account of the events that affected the Florentine Jews summarizes as concisely as possible the literary studies and archival documentation in our possession up to now. I have strictly respected their contents, though the quotations and references have been placed at the end of each chapter for easier reading.

Besides gathering essential information on the subject, this history aspires to be the first contribution to a wider, deeper and more careful treatment of the Jews' connections with the evolving social reality that surrounded them during an important part of our history.

Although aware of these limits, I cannot help but express my emotion in printing this *excursus* which I consider the arrival point of my long years of study on this subject. It has allowed me to come into contact with a reality, with people and with places that, for certain significant aspects, have become part of my life experiences.

For the general bibliography on this subject, I suggest my essay *Breve storia degli ebrei toscani* (Florence: Le Lettere, 1995), pp. 139-162, and also the additional information contained in Michele LUZZATI, "Banchi e insediamenti ebraici nell'Italia centro-settentrionale", in *Storia d'Italia,* Annali 11: *Gli ebrei in Italia* (Turin: Einaudi, 1996) vol. I, p. 194, note 17. In both cases the information refers to all of Tuscany and not just to Florence. Significant publications appearing after 1996 are cited in the text.

I would like to thank the "Centro Editoriale Toscano" of Florence for courteously allowing me to reprint some passages from pages 27-31, 102-106 and 153-163 of one of my essays, *Gli ebrei toscani nell'età della Restaurazione (1814-1848),* published in 1993.

Also a thank you to the publisher, Daniel Vogelmann, and to his wife for the minute by minute attention they paid to the drafting of the text. And a thank you to Ann Curiel, the translator of this English edition, and to Margery Ganz, who reviewed it.

Roberto G. Salvadori

THE JEWS IN FLORENCE: FROM WHEN?

There is good reason to believe that the Jewish community of Florence originated in 1437, the year that some Jewish bankers began lending money there.

As in many other places, the beginnings of a Jewish presence in Florence, while certainly earlier than this date, are obscure and uncertain.

Some scholars hypothesize, with all necessary reserve, that the Jews were already to be found in Florence in the early Middle Ages, while others, though leaving room for doubt, say that their presence goes all the way back to Roman times.

The fact is that the first certain references to Jews coming from Florence appear, strangely enough, in documents that regard other localities where the Jews presumably went on business trips. They concern Eleazaro *from Florence*, found in England in 1286, and a certain Mayr, found in Treviso in 1323.

One year later we come across a *Magister Datillus* (maestro Dattilo, where the name is the Italian translation of Joab). A doctor from Rome, he was in partnership with Ser Cambio Lapi, a pharmacist, with whom he sold medicines in the Oltrarno section of Florence. There was also a certain Manuel de Leone de Urbe from Rome, as the name tells us (and that is all we know).

That there were Jews in Florence between the end of the 13th and the beginning of the 14th century is indirectly proven by the invectives launched against them by Fra Giordano da Rivalto in his sermons held in the Church of Santa Maria Novella and elsewhere between 1303 and 1306. It is difficult to imagine that he was speaking abstractly without referring to local conditions.

Fra Giordano, who bragged that he had learned the *giudesca* language, as he called Hebrew, loved to linger over the subject of the presumed profanation of the holy wafers and images by Jews in Germany. (These accusations were fashionable throughout the Middle Ages and even later.) He also spoke out on the massacres that Christians, indignant over the sacrilege, had perpetrated on the Jews (and here we are much closer to reality). Then, notwithstanding the contradiction, he went on to praise the piety and virtues of the Jews, narrating their conversions in a rather nebulous way.

As far as we know, the Florentine settlement was chronologically the third or fourth one in Tuscany. The first was Lucca, established in the 10th century and very important for its high cultural level. The second was Pisa in the 12th century, while the date of the earliest Jewish presence in Siena is controversial. Until a short time ago it was widely believed that a community (*universitas Judaeorum*) existed there from at least 1229, but that idea was founded on the erroneous interpretation of a document which spoke, instead, of a *universitas Judicum*, that is, a corporation of judges. At any rate it is known that in 1228 a Jew fought in the ranks of the Sienese militia and that a Jewish swindler was condemned to the task of whipping thieves in the city streets.

The nucleus of Jews in Lucca soon lost all organized form, while Pisa, Siena and Florence were destined to welcome true *kehilloth* (communities) that still exist today. The small community of Pitigliano (Grosseto), which has gradually dispersed during the course of the 20th century, and the very important community of Livorno, still in existence with its own particular characteristics, were added in the second half of the 16th century. Another tiny community formed in Monte San Savino (Arezzo), but it had only a brief existence. Established around the middle of the 17th century, it died out in 1799, when a Sanfedist [a reactionary movement opposed to the French revolution] uprising expelled the Jews from the town forever.

Bibliographical note

For further information on the subjects treated here the reference is mainly to Umberto Cassuto, *Gli ebrei a Firenze nell'età del Rinascimento* (Florence: Tip. Galletti e Cocci, 1918; reprinted: Florence: Olschki, 1965), a fundamental text on the history of the Florentine Jews, and not only on them; Robert DAVIDSOHN, *Storia di Firenze* (Florence: Sansoni, 1956), vol. I, pp.196-197; Sofia BOESCH GAJANO, "Il Comune di Siena e il prestito ebraico nei secoli XIV e XV: fonti e problemi", in *Aspetti e problemi della presenza ebraica nell'Italia centro-settentrionale (secoli XIV e XV)*, edited by Sofia Boesch Gajano (Rome [Tivoli: Tipolit. Ripoli], 1983).

THE LOAN BANKS

General Characteristics

In Florence the original nucleus of Jewish settlers consisted of bankers who practiced moneylending, accompanied by their relatives and their employees. They engaged in pawnbroking and to start up their businesses they obviously had initial capital available. It usually derived from the more ample commerce that they had practiced earlier, until they were driven out of those activities by their Christian rivals in the 14th century. What happened in Florence also happened elsewhere: not only in Tuscany but in most of north-central Italy. Between the 1300's and 1400's there was such development that hardly an urban center of any size was without its Jewish bank. If we keep in mind that their owners did not act in isolation but as part of actual companies, obviously in order to provide reciprocal guarantees, we can easily understand how a very close-knit network of banks extended over the whole territory.

Although this phenomenon is well known and carefully as well as profoundly studied, not all the questions on the subject have been fully and satisfactorily answered. It is certain, however, that in that period two stereotypes were created which became the basis of today's anti-Judaism and anti-Semitism. The first one is the sordid Jewish usurer, avid for other people's blood, as depicted in clergymen's sermons of those times. The other, established much later, is the Jewish capitalist, the businessman without scruples or mercy.

There was a period of time between the 11th and 13th centuries in which usury was in Christian hands: Cahorsins, Lombards and Tuscans (though they were mainly interested in large transactions and tended to ignore small loans based on pawned everyday items, which were left to the Jews). The interest set by these lenders was universally very high. In Florence it was 25% on the average, but there was no lack of bankers who asked higher interest rates, up to 66.66%. In the countries to the north of the Alps the percentages were even higher.

The main reason that the Jews had a virtual monopoly on small loans in the late Middle Ages was, as we have said, their progressive exclusion from the types of commerce in which the Christian businessmen, bankers, and financiers were engaged. The Jews belonged to a minority throughout Europe and were in a condition of legal inferiority everywhere. Excluded from the exercise of every trade and profession (with the single partial exception of the medical arts) and forbidden to possess real estate, they were certainly not able to face the competition of the Christians, who were becoming more and more prosperous and ruthless. The Jews fell back on purely monetary activities such as pawnbroking, investing the capital gained from their earlier commercial activities which had been changed into cash.

The negative concept that the society of that epoch had of loaning for interest helped establish the phenomenon. According to their way of thinking, everything that was added to the sum refunded for a loan was considered usury. The prohibition was of ethical-theological origin and is contained, in rather explicit and imperious terms in the Bible and specifically in Deuteronomy: *You may not loan to your brother under any form, but only to the foreigner*. It regarded, therefore, both Jews and Christians, but the latter, citing a passage of the Gospel of Luke (*lend without hoping to make a profit*) assigning to the word *brother* the meaning of *neighbor*, attributed a universal meaning to it and made it an absolute principle.

The object of interminable controversies as far back as the 4th century c.e., the condemnation of usury became more and more resolute over time. Towards the end of the 12th century Pope Alexander III refused the communion sacrament to usurers and forbade them to have a Christian burial. The same treatment was reserved for prostitutes. In 1215, the 4th Lateran Council – which among other things made it obligatory for the Jews to wear a distinctive yellow or red badge – severely prohibited the Christians to join the Jews in usury. The new orders of mendicant friars and preachers – the Franciscans and the Dominicans who were present and working in Florence – in an effort to restore purity to Christian behavior assumed an even stricter position against moneylending and against those who practiced it. And their rebukes found eager listeners among the crowds.

Moneylending, however, in one form or another was an unavoidable necessity, especially in a period like the Middle Ages, when cash was scarce. This was further accentuated by the fact that a closed economy had vanished long before, and money had become, or was once again becoming, the principle means of exchange. Loans were needed not only by the poor people who pawned their few valuable objects to live or to survive – as the texts of that time usually say – but also by the storekeepers, the artisans, and the small merchants for transactions that required immediate payment for merchandise, tools, or raw materials. City governments, including that of Florence, were aware of this fact and tended to allow or at least to tolerate this minor form of money dealing.

Thus a rather complex game was born between the Church, the religious orders, the people and the civil authorities, with various consequences. In this game the Jews were the pawns rather than the players. On one hand, there was the intransigence of the Franciscans and Dominicans, and on the other there was the interest of the secular administrators to use this indispensable economic tool. The ecclesiastic authorities were in a middle position and inclined to search for a compromise: pawnbroking would be forbidden to Christians but tacitly permitted to Jews.

This pattern is evident in the situation of Florence. When the Medici family was in power, Jewish moneylending was allowed and even encouraged. During the periods when the Medici family was forced from power or into exile, Jewish moneylending was prohibited and the Jews themselves were subject to oppressive measures or banished from the city.

In short, loan banking was a service given in concession to, though not imposed on, the Jews in order to liberate the Christians from an unpleasant and thankless job. The Jews – that is, the few of them who had the necessary capital – accepted the role of moneylenders because they had no alternatives. Therefore, it is natural that they tried to profit from the job they were given and that most times they succeeded very well, acquiring more and more experience and capability in managing money along the way, in both the field that the Christians had abandoned and in related areas.

It is impossible to see how Jewish management of loan banks and small businesses – as affirmed in later time – could be considered the premise or even the main source of capitalism, which was such an ample phenomenon that it would require a much wider basis to enable it to appear and become established itself. Pawnbroking was clearly a marginal activity and the Jews' last resort. Beside that, Jewish commerce from the 13th to the 18th centuries was simply wretched (with the sole exception of Livorno from the 17th century on). We are speaking of marginally profitable concessions for the sale of paper, brandy, salt, and later tobacco and, above all, the small-scale commerce of cloth. It was a business that was subjected to constantly increasing limitations (and thwarted by the powerful wool and silk guilds in Florence) to the point that the Jews in the 1600's were allowed to buy and sell only used clothes, remnants, ribbons, etc. This was the *arte degli stracci* [rag trade] mentioned in the Papal Bulls and Cosimo III's orders. The Jews were thus transformed into wandering notions salesmen who went from door to door with a sack on their backs offering their poor merchandise.

The secondary nature of the Jews' moneylending activities is obvious in Florence, which was notoriously one of the most important and flourishing economic centers in Europe in the late Middle Ages. There, in the 15th century, three different types of credit institutions were present: the pawn shops or the so-called panel banks (because the owner had to exhibit a red panel), the small banks and the large banks. The first were given in concession until 1437 to Christians, who were considered public sinners because of their work and subjected to annual fines of two thousand florins which liberated them from the crime committed. As a matter of fact, this fine, formally imposed for ethical and religious reasons, became a tax which benefited the local treasury. From 1437 on past 1496, when the Monte di Pietà [Christian public loan bank] was founded, these banks passed to the Jews. The amount of money handled, though notable, was not even distantly comparable to that of the large banks owned by the Medici, the Strozzi, the Pitti, etc. Even the small banks for the sale of jewels and precious stones had a minor role in comparison to the large banks.

Even the name that was given to Jewish moneylending activity, the *condotta*, indicated the fact that the establishment of a loan bank was the result of reciprocal convenience. It was the rulers of the city that *conducted* the moneylenders into the city, setting precise conditions and requiring very clear guarantees. On the other hand the bank owners, who usually had one or more partners, asked for and obtained particular privileges (please note, privileges not rights) for the entire period of the agreement. The *condotta* generally lasted from three to ten years, though the latter became the norm. These were true contracts, called *capitoli*, written by a notary, often in great detail, and ratified by a resolution of the city council.

Many of the texts of these *capitoli* survive in north-central Italy. Even if they vary in the number of clauses and though some are more detailed than others, they were quite similar over time and space. They naturally contained the names of the contracting parties who were responsible for and guaranteed the observance of the successive clauses. They set the dates for the beginning and the expiration of the *condotta*; they imposed a tax on the bank's activities and set the rates; they established the annual interest rate to be paid on pawns; they set the procedures for handling unredeemed pawns; they obliged the owner to keep accurate registers and account books regarding the bank's operations; they specified the penalties for non-observance of the contract's conditions; they listed the *privileges* (benefits and exemptions) of everyone involved with the bank. Not infrequently they also defined the amount of the initial capital in cash that the lenders had to prove to possess in order to obtain the license. (It went from fifty thousand gold florins – an enormous sum for those times – for a city like Florence to five thousand gold florins for smaller centers).

There was almost always the obligation to lend money only on objects pawned (*ad pignum*) and not on the basis of a written and signed declaration (*ad scriptum, vel ad cartam*). Exceptions to this rule were rare and mainly concerned large loans to public institutions. There were also objects that Jews were not allowed to accept as a pawn, such as objects for ecclesiastical use (from missals to pyx, to vestments, etc.), under penalty of severe fines. Nevertheless, infractions of this clause were not rare.

The owners of the banks were very careful to assure several guarantees for themselves, their families and their employees: first of all to be exempted from wearing the Jews' badge for the whole time of the *condotta*. That was one of the most frequent requests and, at the same time – particularly in certain cities like 15th century Florence – the most difficult to obtain. Then, the right to buy a piece of land to use as a cemetery and, when the conditions were right, to have the use of a synagogue. Frequently there were requests to be protected from harassment and from all ecclesiastical interference, as well as to be exempted from all taxation not mentioned in the *capitoli*. In many cases they expected to be treated as citizens equal to the others especially with regard to legal controversies that might arise, at least for the duration of the contract. The *capitoli* generally closed with a clause establishing that, at the *condotta*'s expiration date, the bank's operations would be easy to close and would be, once again, exempt from harassment.

About twenty people were involved in every bank including five or six owners and partners, the employees, and their families. Thus it frequently happened that in a city where the presence of Jews was not recorded earlier, the group of Jews who took up residence contained at least ten adult males: a *minyan*, that is, the minimum number necessary and sufficient to constitute a community (*kehillah*). The community had a place for prayer and for sacred studies – a synagogue and a school – as well as an internal organization. This first settlement could act as a magnet for other Jews, thus creating the conditions for a lasting presence, but it could also end when the *capitoli* expired.

Jewish Loan Banks in Florence

The most important families of Jewish bankers that settled in Tuscany during the earliest period all came from Rome though their names sometimes carried traces of an intermediate stop: da Camerino, da Rieti, da Terracina. They were all connected to the important da Pisa family, which was also originally from Rome, where its name had been *da Synagoga*. Later, others coming from the north joined them, but those from Rome remained a definite majority: da Montalcino, da Volterra, da San Miniato, da Perugia, da Montepulciano, da Siena, da Pesaro, etc. Often business and even family ties developed among them.

The first evidence of Jewish loan operations in Tuscany goes back to 1309 and concerned the then free commune of S. Gimignano Val d'Elsa, which turned to some Sienese Jews to cover the expenses of an ongoing conflict with Volterra. The negotiations went on for quite a while and probably ended without ever reaching an agreement. Again between 1341 and 1345 the same commune sought Jewish financing, but solid evidence of a *condotta* in S. Gimignano appears only in 1392, forty years after the commune had become Florentine territory.

Florence for a long time was of two minds regarding Jewish moneylending: forbidding it within the city while allowing it outside. The contradiction can almost certainly be explained by the presence of strong Christian loan companies, that were resolute in excluding every rivalry and were willing to profit from the ordinary people's anti-Jewish sentiments for their own purposes. As far as they were concerned, the minor centers, where the volume of business was very small, could be abandoned to Jewish moneylenders.

Starting at the end of the 14th century we come across a series of government (*Signoria*) authorizations for agreements with Jewish companies to establish loan banks in numerous provincial localities: even before the one in S. Gimignano, there was Arezzo (1388), and then Cortona (1404), Colle Val d'Elsa (1406), Pescia (1406), Prato (1406), San Miniato (1406), Castiglion Fiorentino (1407), Montepulciano (1407), Volterra (1407), Castrocaro (1420), Modigliana (1420), Monte San Savino (1421), etc.

Meanwhile, within the city the ethical theological conception that led to the condemnation of moneylending was becoming stronger year after year. In 1396 the hypothesis of bringing the Jews to Florence and obliging them to charge not more than 15% while forbidding Christian moneylending began to be discussed. Nothing came of the discussions. Probably it was simply a threat to induce the Christians to moderate their interest rates. As matter of fact with a statute of 1406, preceded by another deliberation in 1404 and confirmed in 1415 by being inserted in the Statutes, every loan operation by Jews was prohibited and punished by large fines. As a result the few Jews who were found in Florence in this period were not businessmen but mainly doctors. In the first twenty years of the century we find Maestro Salomone Aviçori of Arles, Maestro Leone di Abramo, and Maestro Diamante di Anori enrolled in the doctors' and pharmacists' guild. Jews were also sought to translate commercial and diplomatic documents from Arabic to Latin.

Not only that, but in 1428 Florence was chosen as the site for a convention of important Jews following two other conventions held in Bologna (1416) and Forlì (1418). All these were prompted by Jewish concern over the mendicant religious orders' increasingly violent anti-Jewish preaching and were aimed at obtaining protection from the then-reigning Pope, Martin V.

The atmosphere was right to take up the plan of granting moneylending operations to the Jews even within the city. With an act (*provvisione*) in June, 1430, the *Signoria* was authorized to grant licenses to Jewish bankers, as long as the interest rate was not more than four denari per lira per month (20% on an annual basis). The rate asked by Christians amounted to six denari per lira. The decision was not immediately put into effect but was postponed several times until October 17, 1437, when the *Signoria*, with the consent of Pope Eugene IV, decided to stipulate contracts (*capitoli*) with four loan banks in the name of Abramo, son of Dattilo son of Matassia of the da Pisa family, originally from Rome. In order to undertake such an important job, Abramo – who went under the name of da San Miniato from the town where his family had most recently practiced moneylending – joined with several other Jewish banking families: the da Perugia, da Toscanella, da Tivoli, da Bologna, da Rimini, da Cetona, da Terracina, da Montalcino, etc. It is worthwhile noting that Cosimo de' Medici the Elder, *pater patriae*, had become the true head of the city three years earlier.

The *capitoli* particularly mentioned, among other things:

that said Abramo [di Dattilo da S. Miniato], his partners, his children, his agents, his apprentices and his employees – the group as a whole as well as each one of them – may observe Saturday as a holiday, celebrate all their other holidays as well, and build synagogues, with discretion, according to their laws and their customs [...].

That each and all of them have the right to wear all the clothes and garments they wish, as they like and please, according to their choice and their pleasure, without any badge or other sign beyond or against their will.

But it should be noted that two years later the obligation to wear a badge was repeated for those Jews who did not practice moneylending.

The banks arose in the center of the city. The most important one, called "alla Vacca", "da Panciatichi", was situated among the houses of the Panciatichi family on a street called della Vacca, which now corresponds to the piece of Via de' Pecori that goes from Piazza dell'Olio to Via Brunelleschi. The one called "dei Soldani" was located on the corner of that name on Via dei Neri near the church of S. Remigio. Another was in Palazzo Spini near Ponte S. Trinita, and the last was housed in a building owned by the dei Ricci family on a street that was named after them and is none other than today's Corso between Via dello Studio and Via S. Elisabetta. The dei Ricci bank was later transferred to Chiasso del Borghese in an alley that corresponds to the present Via degli Anselmi.

As already mentioned, it is from 1437 that one can speak of a Jewish community in Florence. The first certain mention of a synagogue's existence dates from 1456, but it is very probable that the Jews who gathered in the city between 1437 and 1438 had already provided for a place of worship.

Settlement was not easy. The Florentine population, as we know, was hostile to the Jews, and pawn brokerage by its very nature was certainly not an activity destined to generate a friendly attitude towards the Jews. The question of the badge (*segno* or *sciamanno*) contributed to increase the Jews' discomfort and discontent. The *capitoli* universally provided for the exemption from wearing the *segno* (an O, that is, a roll of yellow material ten centimeters in diameter, to be worn on the chest or on a shoulder) for all those involved in moneylending activities. So it was for the *capitoli* stipulated in 1437. But already in 1439 the Commune gave a restrictive interpretation to the clause referring to that subject. They repeated that the exemption was only valid for the length of the *condotta* (ten years) and, in contrast to the spirit of the agreement, it added that the exemption was limited to the locality where the bank was situated. Moreover, it pointed out that the exemption would not be included when the contracts were renewed. In 1446 there were new restrictions: the exemption was limited to the bank owner and to two bank employees of his choice. Because of this rule in that year a Jew was fined and imprisoned for not wearing the badge and the intercession of the city's famous bishop, S. Antoninus, was only able to liberate him from prison but did not exempt him from the fine.

When the *capitoli* expired (1448) renewal was particularly difficult because of the question of the *segno*. Finally the Republic had to yield: the moneylenders, their families and their employees were exempted from the *sciamanno*. The obligation to wear it was extremely unpopular with the Jews, who considered it a discriminatory and humiliating measure. Alternating periods of strictness and laxness in applying the law followed, allowing personal exemptions either according to a person's profession (moneylenders and doctors were usually freed from the obligation) or according to whim of the authorities. It took more than three centuries for this oppressive ordinance, shameful for those who imposed it and offensive for those who were subjected to it, to be abolished during Leopold's rule.

In 1450 another company, the da Montalcino, joined the others who had obtained a renewal of their *condotta*. Beginning in 1458 all of them were subjected to a new tax whose revenue went towards the building fund of the church of Santo Spirito. This provision, too, followed a tendency to burden the Jews with the costs of Christian buildings and institutions: a tendency of which there were numerous examples not only in Tuscany but in every part of Italy. The banks continued to be four in number, to the previously mentioned "della Vacca" and "del Borghese" were added "dei Quattro Pavoni" (near the corner where Via dello Sprone meets Via Toscanella) and from 1458 "di S. Pier Maggiore", situated on the corner of Via Torcicoda (where Via Matteo Palmieri meets Via dell'Isola delle Stinche today).

These were particularly difficult years: for the population in general, struck by a plague in 1456-57, and for the Jews in particular. In 1458 the Jews were exposed to the mob's anger after an Observant Franciscan friar of the Visconti family of Milan, preached against them in Santa Croce. The crowd was first calmed by Saint Antoninus, followed by prompt and energetic action on the part of the civil authorities who ordered the friar's immediate expulsion. Thus in the following year the *capitoli* were renewed. As had happened in the past, the Eight of Security and *Balìa*, that is, the authorities in charge of overseeing the loan banks, and from 1478 of overseeing the Jews in general, gave a rather strict interpretation to the agreement. In 1461 Vitale da Montalcino, who had continued his banking activities for a few days beyond the designated deadline, was condemned with the enormous fine of twenty-two thousand florins and to a prison sentence. He was able to leave prison after a few days thanks to the help of Giovanni, the son of Cosimo dei Medici, but he was ruined financially. A similar case had occurred exactly twenty years earlier when Salomone da Perugia was condemned to a twenty thousand florin fine for the illegal exercise of moneylending. The bank, which was officially in his sons' names, had actually been directed by him.

In both cases one suspects that the *Signoria,* wanting to find revenue for the Republic's perpetually empty public coffers, exaggerated in punishing minor infractions or, at least, applied the letter of the law without taking any mitigating circumstances into consideration. In any case, even over and beyond these legal cases, the *condotta* was always accompanied by risks and the chronicles note closures and bankruptcies for simple economic reasons.

It is true, nevertheless, that the customs and the mentality of the times made relations between Jews and Christians difficult. On both sides particular disapproval and severe legal punishment was reserved for mixed sexual relations. In 1434 Guglielmo di Dattilo di Montefalco (who later risked the death penalty for other crimes) was condemned with a fine of five hundred lire for sexual relations with a Christian woman. Between 1463 and 1489 for the same reason four other Jewish bankers were obliged to pay large amounts, which the *Signoria* used for war expenses, for the purchase of Sansepolcro and for the construction of a building to use as its headquarters. Meanwhile, the law on the obligation to wear a badge (which also served to prevent mixed sexual relations) was made stricter (1463). Moreover, it decreed that Jews were allowed to possess holy books only on the condition that they did not contain anything offensive to the Christian religion.

Shortly after the renewal of the *capitoli* in 1471, there were anti-Jewish riots sparked by now-forgotten accusations made by a converted Jew. (The Jews who became Christians obviously felt obliged to distance themselves from their old faith in order to gain greater credibility. They often became their former co-religionists' worst enemies). In 1473 a Monte di Pietà (actually a *Monte di sovvenzione e di carità*, an institution distributing charity and subsi-

dies) was first proposed to substitute Jewish moneylending operations. The project failed for various reasons, one of which was the
fact that the Dominicans refused and condemned every form of interest on money loaned. Four years later, however, all the Jews not
connected to the loan banks were expelled from the city.

Fiery anti-Jewish preaching by the Franciscans – which provoked riots comparable to pogroms almost all over Italy – was
taken up again in Florence between 1487 and 1488 by one of the
most famous preachers on this subject, Bernardino da Feltre. Here
too, at the end of his sermons which were held in the cathedral over
a period of several months, a number of young men turned against
the Jewish loan banks and threatened the life of Manuele da Camerino, called Manuellino, who was saved only thanks to the timely
and firm intervention of the authorities.

And on the day of November 25th, 1487, a friar Bernardino of the Order of St. Francis, who was elected preacher in Santa Maria del Fiore for
the period of Lent, preached and persuaded the people to found a Monte di
Pietà, and to chase out the Jews. He heated up the atmosphere for many
days during Lent and stirred up the young people against the Jews. And in
this day many of these young boys went to the house of a Jew called Ma-
nu[e]llino, who was a moneylender at the Vacca, and they wanted to assas-
sinate him and raid that loan bank. But immediately, the Eight sent their
men to make amends and they issued banns threatening to hang them. And
soon the flareup was extinguished. So that on the 13[th], the other morning,
the Eight sent a messenger to order the friar not to preach any more and
they sent him to the Osservanza [Convent] of Samminiato. But that was not
enough for them, so the next morning on the 14th, which was a Friday in
March, the Eight once again sent both their people and some of the Eight in
person to order him to get out of our country and leave. Whereupon it
seemed to the population that wanted to live a Christian life, that it was a
bad omen for us since he was considered a saint. And in a short time bad
things began to happen [to] some of those Eight: one broke his neck falling
from a horse, and others suffered one thing or another. The one of them
who went in person to chase him out of the convent went crazy and died in
the hospital. It seems he ended badly, God forbid. [Luca Landucci, *Diario
fiorentino dal 1450 al 1516*].

The *condotte* were renewed for the last time in 1491, almost on
the eve of the death of Lorenzo the Magnificent, considered by the

Jews, not without reason, their main protector. Immediately after his death (1492) the atmosphere of hostility against the Jews rapidly increased. Some Jews expelled from Spain arrived in Florence, and since they were all considered Marranos, they were greeted with suspicion by the population. In August of 1493, the young Jew, Bartolomeo de Cases, being guilty of wounding his companion with a small knife during a squabble and – more important – of having damaged some sacred images worshipped by the Catholics (according to his own confession extracted under torture), was condemned to a punishment that today fills us with horror. One of his hands was to be cut off in front of the Madonna of Sant'Onofrio, the other hand before Saint Mary in Campo. His eyes were to be put out in front of Orsanmichele (which contains a plaque in memory of the episode). But the cart that was carrying him to his first punishment was assaulted by the angry populace who stoned the hated Jewish boy to death and then dragged his body for more than fifty blocks while continuing to hit him with sticks. The body was abandoned shortly after Porta Romana, where justice officials took the martyred corpse to perform the sentence ordered by the Eight of Security and of *Balìa*.

And again in the same year, 1493, Bernardino of Feltre returned to preach for a first time in June and a second time in July. Though he came back to his usual anti-Jewish themes only on the second occasion, one cannot exclude the possibility that his words, which increased the hostile feeling already present among the common people, somehow influenced the crowd's actions on that occasion. Later perhaps more severe damage was done to the Jewish loan banks, when, in 1494, a pamphlet by Beato Marco da Monte S. Maria in Gallo was reprinted and distributed *proving* that an initial capital of one hundred ducats at 30% annual interest produced the enormous sum of fifty million ducats in fifty years. The discussion was not based on reality but seemed to use undeniable mathematical reasoning and did much to prove that the Jews were accumulators of limitless wealth.

In addition, there was the preaching of Girolamo Savonarola. The friar from Ferrara had a peculiar personal relationship with Judaism. According to him the Florentines were to replace them as the chosen people in a new covenant, after the earlier one assigned to the Jews by God. Rome was compared to Babylon. Savonarola considered himself at times Noah, the ark builder, or at times Haggai, the prophet who rebuilt the Temple. But on the other hand, in contrast to the Dominican order to which he belonged, he vigorously and concretely supported the idea of a Monte di Pietà in Florence, though in a less fiery tone than preachers like Bernardino da Feltre and the other Franciscans. Once the Medici family, represented by Piero, was expelled from the city in 1494, a Republic was established in which Savonarola had a leading role. In the last days of the following year a provision of the *Signoria* annulled all the *capitoli* stipulated with the Jews and expelled them forever, giving them a year to liquidate their businesses. On April 21, 1496, the Statute of the Monte di Pietà was definitively approved, and Manuele da Camerino helped finance the institution, either out of mere generosity or to keep the Jews from receiving even worse treatment. Actually, because closing the loan bank operations took longer than expected and went beyond the permitted time limit, more than one Jew, for various reasons, remained in the city for the whole Republican period.

In 1512 with the Medici restoration, the Jews were readmitted to Florence, notwithstanding the population's continuing hostility. Two years later the loan banks reopened under the same conditions as were conceded previously. We even find the same names: da Pisa, da San Miniato, da Rieti, da Prato, da Montalcino, da Fano, etc. That the Monte di Pietà was incapable of meeting everyday economic needs was evident. In 1514 the construction fund (Opera) of Santo Spirito asked for the Jewish banks to be taxed in its favor, as they had been a half a century earlier. In 1523 Laudadio da Rieti and Daniele da Pisa lent four thousand florins to the State and in 1524 the *capitoli* were renewed even before they expired.

Three years later the Medici were again expelled along with the Jews. The last Florentine Republic reinstated the measures that were in effect thirty years earlier. That was the definitive end of Jewish moneylending in Florence, although, as on the previous occasion, the expulsion decree was not applied to the letter. As matter of fact, in some cases the Eight itself allowed some Jews to return and reside within the city walls, as in the case of Ismaele da Rieti who had taken refuge in the Mugello Valley, but was treated so badly there that the solution found for his protection was to welcome him back to the city. (He finally found refuge in Siena). The legislation with

regard to the Jews was once again applied in a strict or even perse-
cutory manner. In 1528 Salamon di Ventura, having had sexual relations with a Christian woman, was condemned to perpetual exile,
but first he had to cross the city tied to the back of an ass with a
mitre [ecclesiastical hat] on his head, and he was subjected to whipping, to having his ears cut off and being branded. Jechiel Nissim da
Pisa was accused of having stolen from some Christians. (This time
the trial ended with his absolution). Isaac Tedeschino was condemned for smuggling playing cards, etc.

In 1530 there was the final and lasting restoration of the Medici
family and, consequently, the readmission of the Jews, although not
as moneylenders. Once the Monte di Pietà reopened in 1533, it had
a monopoly on all moneylending and pawn brokerage operations.
Under Cosimo I (1537-1574) the Jews enjoyed his protection until,
between 1569 and 1570, his attitude changed completely and he decreed their confinement in a ghetto. It was the price he had to pay to
Pope Pius V, in order to obtain the title of Grand Duke of Tuscany.

Bibliographical note

On these subjects the fundamental texts of U. Cassuto and M. Luzzati have al-
ready been mentioned. To them must be added, among others: Salo Wittmayer
BARON, *A Social and Religious History of the Jews*, vol. XII (New York and London:
Columbia University Press, 1967); Marino CIARDINI, *I Banchieri Ebrei in Firenze nel
secolo XV e il Monte di Pietà fondato da Girolamo Savonarola* (Borgo S. Lorenzo:
Tip. Mazzocchi, 1907). On the years going from 1512 to 1537: Cecil ROTH, *The Last
Florentine Republic* (London: Methuen & Co., 1925). The passage quoted from the
Capitoli of 1437 is the translation from the original kept in the State Archives of Flo-
rence (*Capitoli*, 100).

JEWISH CULTURE
AND THE FLORENTINE RENAISSANCE

The period of Jewish banking in Florence coincides with that of the city's greatest splendor, when it was a cultural center of unequalled importance, particularly during the time that Lorenzo the Magnificent held power from 1469 until the year of his death in 1492. Arts and letters flourished with the production of an extraordinary quantity of masterpieces. You could almost say that the entire city was overcome by a limitless and unrepeatable creative fever. Florence created a new conception of man, and even more, of the world, universally known as Renaissance humanism.

Between this striking phenomenon – which is so well-known that it hardly needs to be explained – and the Jewish presence in the city there is more than one connection. The very presence of the Jews would not have been possible without the tolerant and even benign attitude of the first Medicis, Cosimo, *pater patriae*, and then his grandson Lorenzo. Besides, Jewish culture itself, while maintaining its own identity, was immersed in such a contagious climate of innovation in every branch of knowledge, that it experienced one of the most important moments in its own development. Relationships with the Christian world arose which were rather complex and not free of contradictions, but certainly enriching.

Recent studies have revealed what was hidden or unknown until a short time ago: the vivacity and variety of Jewish cultural manifestations in many Italian cities in the 15th and 16th centuries, which reached their apex in Florence. It is true that the intensity of debate between different positions (for example between those who followed the Cabala and those who didn't) and between different interests that arose all derived from and aimed at a single goal, the strict adherence to their traditional religion. But it would be surprising if

that were not the case. At that time Jewish identity was completely
bound up with the Jewish religion, and that remained uncondition-
ally true until the end of the 18th century.

In Florence one could meet rabbis, writers, doctors, scholars of
philosophy and physics, translators (mainly from Hebrew, but also
from Arabic and other languages)... In Jewish society much attention was given to widespread literacy, much more so than among
the non-Jews. To know the Torah it was necessary to know how to
read, which necessarily led to knowing how to write. To practice
moneylending it was necessary to know how to do arithmetic, keep
account books, take care of correspondence... And based on this another ambiguous Jewish stereotype was formed: the Jews' greater
intelligence, portrayed as craftiness or sly cunning by their enemies.

Those same bankers who earned their living from moneylending were not men who limited themselves to their daily dealings.
Quite the contrary. They owned libraries of manuscripts (and later
of books) that, considering the times, were of more than considerable size and qualitatively worthy of attention. They participated in
cultural life personally. They wrote, commented, discussed. They
hosted and protected scholars, hiring them as tutors for their children. There was, in short, also Jewish patronage of the arts and culture.

Guglielmo di Dattilo da Montalcino (belonging to one of the
families related to the da Sinagoga, or da Pisa family, who were at
the center of both the financial and the cultural activities in Tuscany) was a banker and a rabbi at the same time. He composed liturgical poetry, studied the Talmud and was fascinated by the
Cabala. This attraction set him in contrast to Judah Messer Leon,
who was critical of the mystical approach. And it is worthy of mention that the confrontation took place at a distance. (Judah Messer
Leon did not live in Florence like his rival, but in Mantua). The
question went beyond the walls of Florence and involved other
people and other cultural centers. The son of Guglielmo da Montalcino, Abramo, was a mathematician. Another rabbi, Mosè di Dattilo,
wrote a comment to the Pentateuch – *The Tree of Life* – in which he
showed a profound knowledge of Aristotle and the works of Mai-
monides. In general the Florentine rabbinate proved itself to be edu-
cated and deeply cultured. One must not forget the intense activity
of the Jewish copyists who transcribed prayer rituals, Bibles, legal

documents and various other things, even precious illuminated manuscripts.

Manuele di Bonaiuto da Camerino – that Manuellino we have already mentioned – was also in correspondence with Judah Messer Leon and with Servadio da Bertinoro, a commentator of the Mishnah (that is, of the Tradition: a part of the Talmud). He himself completed philosophical studies and wrote poetry. Another banker, Bonaventura di Manuel da Volterra, was stimulated by a trip to Palestine to write a diary. Lazzaro da Volterra, son-in-law of Vitale da Pisa, composed liturgical hymns and was in close contact with Jochanan Alemanno, whose influence on Giovanni Pico della Mirandola will be discussed later. Another son-in-law of Vitale da Pisa, David da Tivoli, was interested in philosophy and Cabala and, together with Lazzaro da Volterra, he wrote an elegy in memory of his father-in-law when he died. The correspondence that remains testifies to passionately intense exchanges of news, information, and opinions. Among other things a document found by Cassuto speaks of a group of Florentine Jews who went to Bagno Vignone in the Val d'Orcia, also visited by Lorenzo the Magnificent, to vacation, to enjoy themselves, and to play games and practical jokes. There were even mixed Jewish-Christian groups for learning dancing and singing, for both men and women. Among the men of culture, we must mention the Jewish doctors. Enrolled in the doctors and pharmacists' guild in the 15th century, we find Salomone Aviçori (already named at the beginning of this work), Mosè di Mosè, Leone di Abramo, maestro Allegro, Aleuccio di Salomone di Aleuccio da Arezzo, Manuello Leopardi da Fabriano; and then Lazzaro da Pavia and Samuel Sarfati who were also poets and scholars of Hebrew language and literature.

What took place within the small but lively Jewish Community of Florence was not an isolated phenomenon. All of Italy was overrun by an innovative spirit, by philosophies which looked passionately at the past in order to apply their principles to the present, by an unequalled impetus of artistic creation, and by an involvement in civil life unknown earlier. Everywhere the Jewish communities were involved in and surrounded by this atmosphere, even if their activities stayed in the background since they were a minority, and the protagonists were naturally jealous of their primacy. Elia Del Medigo, giving the first rudiments of the Cabala to Pico della Mirandola, shrouded his activity in a mantle of secrecy, almost turning it into a personal confession, though he was really only revealing the doctrine's content.

The Florentine humanists – and particularly those gathered around the famous Platonic Academy – were strongly attracted to Judaism, or, more precisely, in their philological fever, to the Hebrew language as a vehicle of values that they considered extremely important. As we know, their studies concentrated on classical antiquity. The Greeks and Latins, were considered custodians of a profound knowledge which had to be rediscovered so that man could understand himself better and function better in the society in which he lived. Hebrew culture, and more specifically the Old Testament, went back even earlier. It preceded even the Greeks and Latins and therefore, according to the opinion prevalent at that time, was even more authoritative and more worthy of being known and heeded. Besides, was it not the basis for the Christian religion which followed and proved the Jewish religion true?

It must not be forgotten that all of this cultural ferment occurred within a Christian milieu, even when perspectives and solutions distanced themselves from traditional Catholic dogma. Greek philosophy, Roman history and literature, Hebrew, Chaldean, and even Arabic culture (approached mainly as a mediator for Aristotle's writings) were seen as tools to validate the dominant faith. For the Renaissance, as for Medieval times, the *verus Israel* [true Israel] was the Christian religion. The meeting between these two cultures, each considering the other alien, occurred on a basis in which all integration was impossible, but it produced good results nevertheless. It is necessary to warn that the oft-attempted comparison with the Iberian peninsula's medieval golden age, when there was a fortunate meeting of the Catholic, the Hebrew and the Muslim cultures on the basis of a reciprocal exchange of information and ideas, has precise limits when referred to Italy and Florence.

Marsilio Ficino (1433-1499) and Giovanni Pico della Mirandola (1463-1494) were, without a doubt, the two most important figures in the Florentine philosophical milieu and were also those who paid the most attention to Judaism; but they were not the only ones. They were preceded in the first half of the century by Poggio Bracciolini, Ambrogio Traversari, an important member of the S. Maria degli Angeli monastery, and his disciple Giannozzo Manetti.

The latter's intention to exalt the Christian faith, to which he was profoundly bound, stimulated in him an intense desire to be able to read the Sacred Scriptures in the original in order to better understand their meaning. He turned to a Jew who, during this relationship, ended up converting to Christianity taking the name of Giovanfrancesco di messer Giannozzo Manetti. He was used by the Florentine *Signoria* to read documents in the Hebrew language belonging to the moneylenders. This conversion, which was not unique, is a clear indication of the imbalance that existed between the two cultures, or at least, of the different conditions in which the protagonists found themselves. Besides that, Manetti was the author of an unpublished work by the eloquent title: *Contra Judeos et Gentes* (*Against Jews and Gentiles*). The study of the Hebrew language, which he continued under the guidance of Manuele di Abramo da San Miniato (to whom he taught philosophy in exchange), was used by Manetti to uphold what he considered the merits of the Catholic faith in one of the usual disputes between Jewish and Christian sages, organized on that occasion by Sigismondo Malatesta, the ruler of Rimini, in 1447.

At the center of the Platonic Academy, born thanks to Cosimo de' Medici the Elder, was Marsilio Ficino, the great Platonist and Neo-Platonist scholar, together with Ambrogio Poliziano, Luigi Pulci, and Lorenzo the Magnificent himself, Cristoforo Landino, and, later, the Count della Mirandola. A nearly mortal disease in 1474 led Marsilio to vow to dedicate his work to exalting the religion in which he was born. He absolved his vow trying to demonstrate that Platonic philosophy and Christianity could be reconciled or that they actually converged. His most important work was in fact entitled *Theologia platonica* (1482). An excellent translator from Latin and Greek, he also wanted to learn Hebrew, convinced as Manetti was, that this study would help him to further validate his ideas. Actually he never got beyond the level of using quotes from the Hebrew texts to prove his ideas (and he was not always faithful to the original text).

This limit was of secondary importance, however. His thought was one of the richest and most interesting of the Florentine Renaissance, aimed at creating, as it were, the basis for a universal religion in which philosophical truth coincided with religious truth. It has been rightly said that in this way Ficino moved people's attention from God to man, whose soul became the focal point of the universe, the *copula mundi*: that is, the meeting between spirit and matter, between unity and multiplicity. Reality for him consisted of five stages: body, quality, soul, angel, God. The soul, placed in the middle, tended toward the higher stage without losing contact with the lower one, thus acting as a link between them, stimulated by love (Platonic eros) which raises it from the material world to the spiritual one. In formulating his theories Marsilio Ficino underwent the influence of a Jewish Platonic thinker, Solomon ibn Gabirol, whose Jewish origin was unknown to him.

Elements of Ficino's thought were further developed in the work of Judah Abravanel, perhaps the best known Jewish thinker of modern times. Born in Lisbon on an unknown date between 1460 and 1463, he died between 1520 and 1535, a refugee in Italy as a result of the anti-Jewish persecutions in the Iberian peninsula. A member of the great and powerful Abravanel family, he authored, under the name Leone Ebreo, a posthumously printed work which was widely known in the late Renaissance: *Dialoghi di amore* (*Dialogues of Love*). It has been defined as a metaphysics founded on Plato's (and Ficino's) eros, full of cabalistic and magical themes. One can say that there has never been a greater celebration of love. It is likened to a god, or to God himself, capable of establishing a link (*circulus amorosus*) between all the elements that compose the universe. Leone Ebreo described an ascending path of love that led from the lower levels – the natural and tangible – to the highest level, which was the rational. It was a doctrine that was considered a precursor of Giordano Bruno's thought and, even more, of Baruch Spinoza's intellectual love of God.

The most intense and significant point in the relationship between Judaism and Humanism was reached with Pico della Mirandola, who turned to three scholarly Jews to learn their language: Elia del Medigo, Guglielmo Raimondo di Moncada (Flavius Mithridates) and Jochanan ben Izchak (Giovanni di Isacco) Alemanno. Pico was also friendly with other Jews. One of these, Clemente, converted to Christianity and entered the Dominican convent of San Marco, thanks to Pico's and, so it seems, to Savonarola's persuasion.

Elia del Medigo, originally from Crete, settled in Venice and later was a philosophy professor in Padua, where Pico della Mirandola attended his lessons between 1481 and 1482. Perhaps with some exaggeration, Del Medigo declared himself to be an expert in Cabala, a subject that greatly interested the Count of Mirandola. It is certain that he knew the Hebrew translation of Averroes' writings very well and was one of his followers. He even accepted Averroes' theory of the double truth of philosophy and religion. Pico asked him insistently to translate those texts into Italian and called him to Florence several times for that purpose. Together with Guglielmo Raimondo di Moncada and others, Del Medigo took part in the debates between Jews and Christians organized in order to disprove the doctrine of the Synagogue while bringing about the triumph of Christian *truth*. Even Marsilio Ficino had participated in some of these disputes which had become so frequent as to be considered almost a ritual.

Although Elia del Medigo represented a way for Pico to approach Averroes' philosophy by means of translations and Hebrew commentaries, his most important language teacher was Guglielmo Raimondo di Moncada, a Sicilian Jew, who had converted to Christianity and assumed the name Flavius Mithridates. Not much is known about him. He was a scholar of the Cabala, and as such, without a doubt left a profound impression on his illustrious and learned student. Thanks to Mithridates, Pico mastered a good deal more Hebrew than Marsilio Ficino did.

Lastly, the most important relationship of all was with Jochanan Alemanno, who actually became his collaborator. Notwithstanding his name, Alemanno [German], he was born in 1435 or later in Italy in Città di Castello and was of French origin. He was closely connected to the family of Vitale da Pisa where he later tutored the banker's children, Samuele and Isacco. He was in Florence several times, occasionally for long periods: from 1455 to 1462, in 1481, and from 1488 (when he met Pico) to 1494. He also fervently admired the city's organization. Among his writings which were the result of his philosophical discussions with Pico and with Marsilio Ficino, two are particularly worthy of mention: his commentary to the Song of Songs (*L'amore di Salomone*) in which Solomon is presented as a model of encyclopedic knowledge, and *L'immortale*, where – once again – the theme was the ascent of man toward God by means of virtue. It is notable that Alemanno's son, Isacco, taught Hebrew to Giovanni Gian

Francesco, Pico's nephew and a convinced follower of Savonarola, with whom Pico, too, felt an affinity.

With all the fervor of his passionate temperament, the Count of Mirandola embarked on an ambitious plan. He wanted to reach the very roots of universal truth which were, in his opinion, the foundation of human knowledge in the fields of both religion and philosophy. Thus he would establish what he called a *pax philosophica.* He firmly believed to have found the solution to his problem in ancient magic and above all in Jewish mysticism and Cabala. His knowledge of the latter was due more to Alemanno than to Del Medigo and Flavius Mithridates. His *Apologia,* written in 1487, after he failed in his plan to discuss the 900 theses supporting his beliefs in Rome, contains a *Quaestio quinta, de magia naturali et cabala Hebreorum* [Fifth question, on natural magic and Jewish Cabala]. The very title demonstrates how great the influence of Jewish culture was on his thought.

His philosophy moved toward a universalistic idea that the Catholic Church perhaps justifiably considered suspicious, if not actually heretical. It seemed to deprive the *Christian truth* of its distinctive characteristics, allowing it to be engulfed in a philosophical and magical ambience in which it risked being completely dissolved. Affirmations that nothing better than magic and Cabala could demonstrate the divinity of Christ could not have been easily accepted in Rome. Pico was banned from the Church and fled to Paris. Later he was put into prison, but he managed to escape and find refuge at the court of Lorenzo the Magnificent until his early and dramatic death.

And yet what still survives of him today is exactly that message of dignity and liberty addressed to all men, Jews and Christians alike (today we might say believers and non-believers). It is condensed in these words cited in almost every history of philosophy and is still worth repeating:

> I have given you, oh Adam, neither a fixed place, nor an appearance of your own, nor any function peculiar to you, so that you might have and possess that place, that appearance, and that function that you desire, according to your judgement and decision. The limited nature of the other beings is contained in the laws I have prescribed. You, unconstrained by any barrier, will determine your own nature according to your free will, in whose power

I have placed you. I have set you at the center of the world so that from there you could better be aware of all that is in the world. I have made you neither heavenly nor earthly, neither mortal nor immortal, so that as an almost free and sovereign agent, you could shape and fashion yourself in the form that you choose. You may descend to lower, brutish forms of life; or you may, according to your will, rise to superior levels, which are divine.

Bibliographical note

Besides Cassuto, op. cit, see: Roberto BONFIL, *Jewish Life in Renaissance Italy* (Berkeley: University of California Press, 1994), containing an ample bibliography on the subject; Eugenio GARIN, "L'umanesimo italiano e la cultura ebraica", in *Storia d'Italia*, Annali 11, vol. I, op. cit., pp. 359-383; Arthur M. LESLEY, "Il richiamo agli 'antichi' nella cultura ebraica fra Quattro e Cinquecento", ibidem, pp. 385-409; *La cultura ebraica all'epoca di Lorenzo il Magnifico*, edited by Dora Liscia Bemporad and Ida Zatelli (Florence: Olschki, 1998). The quotation from Pico della Mirandola was taken from his *Oratio de hominis dignitate*, I, fol. 314.

THE GHETTO

In Florence the ghetto – or the Ghetto Block – was established in 1571, as a consequence of Cosimo I de' Medici's decision, made in the previous year, to require all the Tuscan Jews living in various localities to concentrate in areas reserved especially for them in Florence and Siena. It was modeled on the ghettos that had been established in Venice in 1516 and in Rome in 1555. Earlier the Florentine Jews had lived not far from the Ponte Vecchio on a street in the Oltrarno district that was thereafter called Chiasso dei Giudei (today, Via de' Ramaglianti). According to an undocumented tradition, the first synagogue of Florence was probably situated on that street, at the corner of Borgo San Jacopo, starting from 1430 when the Jews were allowed to settle in the city.

The job of planning a Florentine Jewish quarter was assigned by Cosimo and his son Francesco to Bernardo Buontalenti. He chose the center of the city where high crenellated walls surrounded the brothels, amidst the porticos and towers that had belonged to the most illustrious noble families such as the Della Tosa, the Tosinghi, and the Arrigucci until the 15th century. Some of the houses of prostitution had been the property of the Brunelleschi, of the Pecori, and even of the Medici. The ghetto occupied a rectangle of about one hundred by two hundred meters, corresponding today (after its demolition in the last twenty years of the 1800's) to the area between Piazza della Repubblica, Via Brunelleschi, Via dei Pecori and Via Roma. The heart of the quarter became the *Cortacce* (thus called with a clear reference to the squalor of the courts and plazas), where earlier, opposite the Church of S. Maria in Campidoglio, had stood the *Gran Postribolo* [the Great Brothel], also called *la Palla* [the Ball], whose construction on top of Roman ruins went back to 1328.

The ghetto consisted of a maze of narrow and dark winding alleys that opened onto two squares joined by an arch. One was the square of the Fountain, the center of the so-called Old Ghetto, and the other was the Brotherhood Square, center of the New Ghetto (an addition ordered by Cosimo III in 1704). The latter had only one entrance from Piazza dell'Olio behind the archbishopric. The other could be entered both from the ghetto's most important street where the most of the Jewish shops were, Via della Nave (corresponding to today's Via dei Tosinghi where it is a continuation of Via dell'Oche), or from the Piazza del Mercato [the Market Square]. Sculpted on the main portal were the coat of arms of Cosimo I and his son Francesco along with the inscription that emphasized how benevolent they had been to welcome the Jews there, rather than chasing them out of the State as they deserved. The translation reads:

> Cosimo dei Medici, Grand Duke of Tuscany, and his Son, the Most Serene Prince Francesco, moved by great mercy for all, wanted the Jews enclosed in this place, separate from the Christians but not expelled, so that they could, through the example of good men, subject their stiff necks to the light yoke of Christ. Year 1571.

Giuseppe Conti, writing at the end of the 1800's in his *Firenze vecchia* defined the Florentine ghetto in its last years as "a remnant of medieval barbarity". He left us a lively and fascinating description, rich in color and interesting details (unfortunately without naming his sources) which has been widely used from his time on. Some passages deserve to be cited in their entirety:

> The inside of the ghetto was as dirty and foul as can be. The city did not make the necessary repairs, the sewers were not cleaned, no one superintended cleanliness or hygiene; and everyone did as he wanted. There were even houses of eleven floors: those built on the wall of the Great Brothel, opposite the Palla. [...]
> In the ghetto there were also rich families; but one could see among the poorer classes the yellow faces of people who breathed unhealthy air, slovenly girls in slippers and uncombed kinky black hair that indicated their oriental origin. The older ones, the mothers, wore wigs, because of a reli-

gious custom that forbid married woman to keep their own hair, so as not to arouse desire in other men. Then there were the half-naked boys that played in the squares and on the stairs covered with a dense layer of black dirt composed of mud and manure accumulated over the centuries. At the windows of all the apartments hung rags, stockings, skirts, sheets full of patches, all gray and dirty looking though they had just been washed.

The Ghetto appeared like a small walled city. It had a separate life, with its own habits and different customs. From Piazza dell'Olio one proceeded along that sort of passage that led to Via della Nave, where draper's and clothing shops sold wares wholesale to the country people. Batiste and coarse cotton fabrics were surrounded by rosaries, crucifixes, soaps and an infinite number of other things that the Jews sold at very low prices. In 1826 there was an epidemic of bankruptcies. Businesses collapsed like cards, and a local wit, moved by this, wrote a song that had the following chorus, "What a scourge, Stenterello – desolated your business!" The Stenterello referred to in the song was a delicatessen owner. [...]

It was curious to see many of these Jews leave the Ghetto in the morning, two or three at a time wearing backpacks, to go to the countryside or from door to door selling sheeting [*ghinea*], kerchiefs of Aleppo [*pezzuole*], Dutch linen, and batiste. Most of them sold on credit and had fixed customers to whom they sold on weekly payments. And if the buyer wasn't punctual in his payments, the Jew was punctual in going to collect his money!...

In most cases they were poor homes, or often really hovels, but in the general desolation one could also find apartments defined as "comfortable and elegant, decorated with uncommon luxury", located on the north side of the ghetto between Via della Nave and the Archbishopric as Guido Carocci wrote in his *Il ghetto di Firenze e i suoi ricordi* in 1886. It was not lacking curiosities such as "a certain Lilliputian dwelling with such a low ceiling that not even a very short person could stand up in it. It was a lair for robbers and vagabonds situated near Via della Nave".

Even the earliest *capitoli* that we have from the Florentine ghetto (from 1595 and discovered by Umberto Cassuto) confirm that the problems that the *massari* [the administrators of the Jewish community] – an elected office from 1608 – had to face were numerous. The measures taken speak clearly: orders to remove piles of fallen plaster and earth that blocked the streets; orders not to set up stands outside the shops ("many times if you want to go by you have to wait for them to let you pass"); orders not to argue and not to play *alla palla, pallone o pallottole* [ball]; prohibition to give nicknames; prohibition to flaunt luxurious clothes; etc.

Even relations with the Christians must not have been easy, since orders and proclamations not to molest the Jews were periodically reissued. The first of these *gride* [proclamations] goes back to 1567, when the ghetto had not yet been established, but Cosimo I had already begun his anti-Jewish policy. Those of 1607, 1639, 1668 (that also forbid taking their children away from the Jews with the "excuse of wanting to lead them to the Sacred Christian Faith"), as well as those of 1735 and 1753 all refer to it.

The sad conditions of the Florentine ghetto were doubtlessly due to overcrowding, as well as the authorities' neglect. We do not know how many people it contained when it was founded, though we do know that the Tuscan Jews in 1571 were slightly more than 700 all told. Data on how they were divided between Florence and Siena are missing, though it is easy to presume that the former contained many more than the latter. (Perhaps there were five hundred in Florence and the rest in Siena, as we are led to believe by the fact that, according to some sources, there were 495 Florentine Jews about a half a century later). Then the number grew until it reached more than 1,500 shortly before the unification of Italy. The area available, however, remained fundamentally the same and became more and more insufficient, even though some rich Jewish families were able to obtain the privilege of living outside the ghetto. (The enlargement decreed in 1704 aimed at bringing those families back). For this reason there were houses of nine and ten floors, raised roofs, additions, distortions of the already old and feeble urban fabric, that only a few surviving illustrations can show us.

Obviously synagogues also stood in the ghetto. Carocci speaks of "two main temples, one with the Italian rite and the other with the Levantine rite, a brotherhood or minor temple that was used for daily services, a funeral brotherhood, rooms for the benevolent society, schools, dancehalls and meeting rooms, baths, butchers, ovens, grocery stores, clothing and homewares stores: everything, as a matter of fact." The Italian rite synagogue was probably founded in 1572 and the Levantine or Spanish rite synagogue in 1596. A fire that devastated the ghetto in 1670 spared the two synagogues.

The synagogues (whose buildings had been sold to the Florentine Jewish Community in 1750) were destroyed along with the rest of the ghetto at the end of the 1800's, in an urban renewal project for the city center. They were substituted by the Sephardi Great Synagogue in 1882, and two years later two small Italian rite synagogues were added. Both were situated at number 5 of Via dell'Oche. In one of these after the Second World War, the Ashkenazi rite was adopted in order to satisfy the religious needs of those who, coming from beyond the Alps, had settled in Florence. It was called *Mattir Asurim,* from the name of the ancient brotherhood whose purpose was to pay the ransom money to free Jews from prison.

The cemetery was situated in San Frediano, a lower-class neighborhood of the Oltrarno area. This placement was perhaps connected to the earliest years of Jewish settlement, which, as we have already seen, took place in the southern part of the city. When in 1835 that cemetery became insufficient, the *massari* of the Florentine Jewish community asked for a piece of land next to the Christian cemetery of Trespiano. The city council unanimously refused the request with the motivation that "if conceded, it could arouse universal discontent in the Catholic Population". Between the end of the 1800's and the beginning of the 1900's, the old cemetery near Porta Romana was substituted by the present one in Via di Caciolle.

The request made by the Florentine Jewish community in 1833 to allow poor Jewish girls to be granted marriage dowries on the occasion of the Grand Duke's wedding was also refused by the city's Gonfaloniere [mayor]. According to him, it was a French custom that should not be continued. And yet the *Nazione Ebrea* [the Jewish community of that period] had not forgotten to manifest its joy for the sovereign's wedding, and above all, it had not forgotten the satisfaction expressed by Ferdinand III, the father of the reigning Grand Duke, for the community's decision to set aside four thousand lire to be shared among poor Christian girls on the occasion of his "happy return" to the throne in 1814.

The function of the ghetto was to keep the Jews separate from the Christians as much as possible; to keep the former from leaving it and the latter from entering it at night. (The job of closing the gates at midnight and reopening them at dawn was given to a Jewish gatekeeper.) But this function began to loose importance during the reign of the House of Lorraine in 1755. Not that explicit measures were taken, but the authorities simply stopped their inspections. The obligation to close the gates tacitly ended, but the Jews continued to fulfil this duty on their own for 80 years more.

On December 20th, 1778, Peter Leopold, almost as a seal of approval for this autonomy, decided to auction off the whole ghetto to the highest bidder. The first auction was deserted, but at a later one the Jews Jacob Bassano of Livorno, Angelo di Vita Finzi, and the two Rimini brothers David Salomone and Moisè Vita of Florence were present as buyers. The contract was written by the Notary Marco Gaetano Tosi on June 9th, 1779, on the basis of 34,584 *scudi* (10,000 of which to be paid immediately and the rest in twelve yearly payments).

At the end of 1834 the *Consiglio Israelitico* [the Jewish Council] finally decided not to continue closing the three gates of the ghetto (two at midnight and another less important one at noon), arousing the protests of 39 Jews. They reminded the Council as a warning that "the gates provided security for the houses, shops and schools". The police were even asked to intervene, but they were perplexed and declared their incompetence, leaving the police station of S.M. Novella to untangle the question. The *Consiglio* wrote a Memorandum illustrating its point of view. The document mentioned that though it was the need to cut expenses, including the doorkeeper's salary, that had created the opportunity, they also claimed the Jews' right to abandon a custom that recalled periods of humiliation and shame. The 8th of January, 1835, the ghetto gates stopped being shut and were permanently attached to the side walls. On the 14th of February the *Buongoverno* (the police of those times) let it be known that they had no objections. The segregation-separation of the Jews was finally completely ended.

Bibliographical note

Please see my essay, already quoted, *Breve storia degli ebrei toscani*, my personal research in the archives, and moreover, Umberto CASSUTO, "I più antichi capitoli del ghetto di Firenze", in *Rivista Israelitica*, IX (1913) and X (1913); Giuseppe CONTI, *Firenze vecchia* (Florence: R. Bemporad e Figlio, 1900); Guido CAROCCI, *Il ghetto di Firenze e i suoi ricordi* (Florence: Tip. Galletti e Cocci, 1886); Osanna FANTOZZI MICALI, *La segregazione urbana. Ghetti e quartieri ebraici in Toscana: Firenze, Siena, Pisa, Livorno* (Florence: Alinea, 1995); Giampaolo TROTTA, "Cimiteri ebraici a Firenze", in *Storia urbana*. XVI, 59 (April-June 1992), pp. 127-151; Dora Liscia Bemporad, "La scuola italiana e la scuola levantina nel ghetto di Firenze: prima ricostruzione", in *Rivista d'Arte*, XXXVIII, serie IV, vol. II (1986), pp. 3-48.

THE PERIOD OF THE COUNTER-REFORMATION
THE HOUSE OF THE CATECHUMENS

The Church in the period of the Counter-Reformation tried persistently to have the Jews convert to Catholicism, using every possible means to reach its goal. Calm and reasonable persuasion, interwoven with theological arguments, was accompanied and often supplanted by urgent pressure. Enticements, wheedling, promises of better social and economic conditions, suspension of prison sentences and even of death sentences, nothing was overlooked in an effort to get the Jews to convert. Not even the use of violence was lacking. An example of this was the forced sermons for which the Jews were obliged to gather in a church on Sundays in order to listen to the reprimands of a friar who was often a converted Jew. He generally specialized in accusing the Jews of being stiff-necked for not wanting to recognize the truth of Christianity, and he usually urged them to open their eyes, to repent and to change their faith. And finally there was the conversion imposed on Jewish children, who were taken away from their families with various excuses. The most common instance was the baptism of a newborn Jewish baby, believed to be in mortal danger, by a Christian housemaid. It was sufficient to learn of the housemaid's act for the Church to seize the child in order to educate him in the Christian religion and often push him into the priesthood. The Church celebrated the baptism of a converted Jew as a triumph and tried to give the event the maximum publicity.

From the mid 16th century special institutions for the conversion of non-Catholics (and most particularly of the Jews) to Christianity began to be established everywhere, starting in the Papal States. Among these institutions the House of the Catechumens [people being instructed in the fundamentals of the Catholic religion] was especially important. It was intended to welcome those who had expressed their intention to be baptized and to receive the rudiments of Christian doctrine.

The origin of the house of the catechumens of Florence went back to 1636 when a Carmelite friar from Mantua, Alberto Leoni, founded a Brotherhood in Florence composed of well-born men and women dedicated to converting the Jews to Christianity. On the 28th of November of that year the archbishop, Piero Niccolini, approved the statute. The Brotherhood, supported by Grand Duke Ferdinando II de' Medici, bought two small houses on Via Palazzuolo and welcomed the first catechumens. However, this initial experiment encountered difficulties, and though it seems to have ended after a short time, it aroused much alarm among the Florentine Jews. The community turned directly to the Grand Duke, sending him a formal petition that was midway between a protest and a request:

> Most Serene Grand Duke – The Jewish Nation of Florence, the humblest servant of His Serene Highness, humbly reminds Him that for more than one hundred years they were and are under the shadow and protection of the Very Serene House of Medici and were never placed under the jurisdiction of any other court except that of their Highnesses. Now some orders and laws have been permitted to be drawn up against it by the Deputies over the Catechumens. The Jews turn to the benevolence of His Serene Highness begging not to allow the aforementioned supplicants to be burdened nor subject to new laws and orders issued by anyone except the usual Magistrates to which they are normally subjected by law.

The initiative arose again under Cosimo III, pious to the point of being considered more than a bigot, a religious maniac. Favoring the conversion of the infidels was a point of honor and a glorious deed as far as he was concerned. Therefore, he began to subsidize the neophytes so generously that "to become Catholic in Tuscany had become a kind of speculation", as Passerini, a historian of the benevolent societies of Florence who we will quote again shortly, wrote in the 1800's. The number of converts – Jews, Muslims, and schismatics – began to grow once again. Solemn processions of catechumens marching toward the Baptistry with a banner in their hands became frequent. They recalled the famous procession ordered by Cosimo I in 1551 in which eighteen Jewish children from

Rome, after being taken from their parents and dressed in red, were made to parade through the streets of Florence for the edification of the citizens and for the glory of the Christian religion. Many of these conversions were obviously false, and it sometimes happened that a new Christian, when at death's door, returned to invoking the God of Abraham, Isaac, and Jacob, turning his head towards the wall according to the Jewish custom in front of a scandalized Christian confessor.

It is perhaps significant that the first Jewish convert of those coming from the Florentine house of catechumens for which we have documents immediately took advantage of his new state in January of 1651 to ask for and obtain the authorization to contract a new marriage (since his earlier Jewish marriage was considered annulled).

Donations by the sovereigns, the participation of noble Christian families, and bequests all contributed to the prosperity of the house of the catechumens. The two narrow buildings on Via Palazzuolo (perhaps one for men and the other for women) were substituted, in 1716, by a larger building on Borgo Pinti, the Convent of the Angiolini, in use until 1792. In that year the catechumens were transferred to the presbytery of S. Michele Visdomini, on the Via dei Servi, and finally from there, after Fernando III's return in 1814, to a part of the ex-convent of the women Cavaliers of Malta, on Via San Gallo. It began functioning, however, only in 1821. From August 26th, 1791, the institution had been put under the jurisdiction of the Commissar of Bigallo, whose main job, however, was to take care of orphans.

From that year on, the practice of admitting people to the house of the catechumen remained the same. The Commissioner of Bigallo accepted the requests to be admitted and asked for the intervention of the *Buongoverno* (as already mentioned, this was the name used to indicate the Tuscan police). They were to gather information on those who wanted to become Christians (age, profession, residence, marital status, economic conditions, but mainly moral conduct, family situation, the reason for wanting to become Christian, and the trust-worthiness of the intentions expressed). The *Buongoverno* then transmitted the request to the commissars of the neighborhood, whose replies followed the reverse path. The report of the commissars was usually decisive. If it was favorable, the applicant could enter the catechumens, where he remained for instruction in Catholic doctrine for forty days. At the end he would usually be baptized. For women there was a slight variation: they were accepted to the house on Via San Gallo as soon as they applied and were held there on deposit until the information on them was received. Besides offering general protection and hospitality to the weaker sex, the measure was clearly aimed at helping young women to escape from their homes when it was feared that their parents or their relatives would make them return.

Once the person entered, the *Jewish Nation* was notified, and information on the applicant was requested from the Chancellor. The representatives of the Jewish community and the person's closest relatives were allowed to meet with him once in order to receive an explanation. This meeting took place in the presence of the Commissioner of Bigallo or his delegate (usually the director of the house of the catechumens – a priest) and, by law, it had to be free. That is, the relatives of the catechumen had the right to test his will, using whatever reasons they wished to change his mind. Later meetings were possible, but only if the catechumen agreed.

The catechumen's living expenses were charged to his family or to the *Jewish Nation,* which had to pay in advance the sum necessary for the entire period of his instruction. If the catechumen reached baptism, the sum was returned; otherwise it was taken by the institution but only for the number of days the person remained there. The normal stay was considered to be forty days, except in cases of mortal danger. A provision passed on December 19th, 1827, set the stay in the house at forty days, and the down-payment to be given by the Jewish community as a guarantee of the result of the proselytizing process was set at 80 lire (two lire a day).

The rule of allowing a face to face meeting between the catechumen and his relatives as a guarantee of free choice was scrupulously respected by the authorities. The jurisdictionalist tradition initiated under Leopold was still in effect in this case. Other rules, on the other hand, were subject to various interpretations according to the cases. The one most often disregarded was the imposition of at least a forty day stay. Numerous controversies arose with the Jewish community, interested in the rigorous application of the principle of a guarantee against secret or forced baptisms. Often the opposite happened, the catechumen's stay went beyond the anticipated minimum time.

To become a catechumen and then a neophyte, it was necessary to be at least thirteen years old: this limit coincided with the Jewish custom of coming of age. The baptism of non-Christian minors and particularly of infants was forbidden if done without the parents consent. The person who imparted baptism was considered guilty of a crime and subjected to a trial. (As already mentioned, usually it regarded wet nurses and Christian servants working in Jewish families. Imbued with candid religious fanaticism, they sometimes baptized the baby secretly convinced that they were doing a good thing for the child). At any rate, though illegal from a judicial point of view, the sacrament was considered valid from a theological point of view. Remember that according to Christian doctrine, the "minister" of baptism "in case of necessity could be anyone, even a heretic or an infidel, as long as he had the intention to do as the Church does". Moreover baptism by itself impressed the character of Christianity indelibly, whether or not the baptized person accepted to consider himself Christian as an adult. Thus differences arose between civil and ecclesiastical authorities, which were solved in various way according to the circumstances.

Once accepted the catechumens could not be molested; that is, even their closest relatives had to stay away from the building where they were staying. In 1786, for example, when the street around the Convent of the Angiolini was being repaired, it was necessary to find a way to avoid having Jews pass in front of the building.

The institution of the catechumen lasted longer than one would think for the Florentine Jews. The last case for which there is still evidence goes back to September, 1867, six years after the unification of Italy. The house at that time had been transferred to Via degli Alfani.

An estimate of the results obtained by this work of conversion is not easy. The number of documented cases in which Jews asked to be taken into the house of the catechumens of Florence in the course of two centuries (from the mid 1600's to the mid 1800's) was less than 150. To that number must be added those whose conversion took place outside official channels and about which, therefore, we have no information. It is probable that they were only a few dozen, or possibly less than a dozen. On the other hand, those who asked to be admitted as catechumens but did not finalize their decision and continued in their original faith must be subtracted from the total. At the end, we must return to the approximate figure previously indicated.

The cases of Jewish babies taken away from their families because they had been secretly baptized against their parents' will were relatively rare, particularly in Florence: six or seven, documented between the 17th and 18th centuries – none in the 19th century. But elsewhere – in Livorno and above all, in southern Tuscany, Siena and Pitigliano – this custom was still present in the 19th century. The last known case, regarding an under-aged girl in Pitigliano goes back to 1861; therefore, three years after the Mortara case, which took place in the Papal States and was famous for Pope Pius IX's intransigence in refusing to return the child to his family, notwithstanding the pressure brought to bear on all sides.

It is evident, from what has been said about the specific question of the conversion of the Jews, that the saddest period for the Florentine Jewish community was between the end of the 17th and the beginning of the 18th centuries, which coincided with the long reign of Cosimo III de' Medici (1670-1723). For example, a measure decided in 1649, but not immediately enforced, was confirmed and made even stricter in 1678. It excluded the Jews from their main commercial activities: the sale of locally produced and imported fabrics, notions (lace, ribbons and floss-silks), gold, silver and silk buttons, gold and silver objects, and precious stones (except for unpolished ones):

> And in short these Jews cannot keep in the City any sort of new merchandise of the type belonging to the silk workers, the wool workers, the goldsmiths, the goldbeaters, the drapers, the notions makers, the veil makers and all other goods pertaining to the guilds. But they are only permitted to keep and sell old and used objects.

Because of intertwining corporate interests and religious prejudices shared by the sovereign, it was also forbidden to the Jews to act as middlemen for this merchandise. We can easily understand what a harsh blow that was to their economic resources.

In those same years restrictive and humiliating measures regarding all of the Jews of Tuscany followed one another continually: prohibition for Christians to work as servants in Jewish households (1677 and 1718); prohibition for Jews to employ Christian wet nurses (1677 and 1683); prohibition of cohabitation between Jews and Christians (1680); prohibition of carnal commerce between Jewish men and Christian women and vice versa (1677, 1678, 1679 and 1680). The punishments prescribed were particularly rigorous and increased in severity from one proclamation to the next for people guilty of the last misdeed. The proclamation of 1679 stated the following:

> The Most Serene Grand Duke of Tuscany, and for His Serene Highness, the Illustrious and Notable Deputy and Keepers of the Florentine Republic, have provided, ordered and commanded that if any Jew in whatever state, grade and condition should be found inside habitation of a prostitute or harlot, he will be fined 300 *scudi*, and the said prostitute or harlot will be fined another 300 *scudi*, and if one or the other is unable to pay the fine completely or in part, he will be condemned unconditionally to three stripes of the cord in public for the Jew and to prison, according to the will of His Highness, for the prostitute or harlot.

Similar punishments were foreseen in the opposite case (a Christian man with a Jewish woman). The punishments were made more severe in the case of relapses (besides a fine, there were prison sentences, whipping, etc.). In the cases of rape the death sentence was prescribed. Similar measures opened the door to grotesque tricks, such as *illaqueamento* (today we would say enticement). It could happen that a prostitute would attract a Jew into her house or even push him in, and then a policeman with whom the woman had an agreement would catch them. Of course, the policeman would receive a percentage of the fine.

In this climate it is not surprising that the Jews lived in constant fear, so that in 1678 the *massari* were induced to order that *Purim* (which fell during Lent that year) be celebrated very quietly, so as not to provoke the foreseeable abusive reactions by the Christians.

Nor was there a lack of problems within the community. Disagreements between the Italian Jews and those of Levantine origin were settled only in 1688, on the basis of an agreement that provided for a single community with separate synagogues. In some things Jewish morality at that time was no less restrictive and obtuse than that of the Christians. Relations between Jews and Christians were condemned by the community in no less harsh tones than those already mentioned. The *massari* severely prohibited the Jewish women every minimum luxury in dress, etc.

In the life of the more and more miserable and impoverished ghetto very few breathing spaces remained. Some of the Jews, squeezed out of the fabric trade, took on various types of concessions: tobacco, salt and paper, schnapps, which at the time were treated as monopolies. Some even found a way to become rich, as happened in the case of Salomone Levi, from Mantua, whose patrimony was estimated at one hundred thousand Florentine *piastre*.

With the successor of Cosimo III, Gian Gastone (1723-1737), an unruly and indolent but more tolerant sovereign, the condition of the Jews in Florence and Tuscany became more bearable. However, greater freedom would be available to them only after Francis I of the House of Lorraine was installed in office. His entry into Florence in 1739 was welcomed by great celebration on the part of the Jewish community too. A *machine* [a stage set] prepared for the occasion made a big impression:

The machine made by the Jews was 38 arms high [more than 22 meters] and included the coat of arms of His Highness in two great pictures painted and set over the arches of the machine. It was situated on four corners: the one in front of the Cathedral, the one in Piazza dell'Olio, the one toward S. Maria Maggiore and the one that leads to Piazza Madonna. It was composed of four triumphal arches supported by 16 beautiful architectural columns. Above each there was a statue that denoted Clemency, Justice, and in short all that which usually appertains to a Prince. At the foot of the said columns were other statues equal to those above and over each arch a Latin motto, and all was very well illuminated. And when His Highness passed underneath, a number of musicians with every sort of instrument were set on a platform.

Bibliographical note

On the question of conversions and of the House of the Catechumens please see my essay *Gli ebrei toscani nell'età della Restaurazione (1814-1848)* (Florence: Centro Editoriale Toscano, 1993), containing the quotations cited here.

THE REIGN OF LEOPOLD AND THE FRENCH PERIOD

During the enlightened government of Peter Leopold of Hapsburg-Lorraine (1765-1790), the condition of the Tuscan Jews (and therefore also of the Florentine Jews) began to change substantially. The Sovereign had no prejudice against them and greatly appreciated their industriousness and their spirit of initiative, particularly in the commercial sector which he wished to develop and liberalize. Moreover, a part of the clergy (though a small minority, whose main representative, the bishop of Pistoia and Prato, Scipione de' Ricci, was close to the Grand Duke) had assumed a different attitude toward the Jews than the one traditionally held by the Catholic Church. Jansenism, full of moral rigor and desire for reform, tended to underline the continuity between Judaism and Christianity rather than their contrasts.

As we have seen, the closure of the ghetto had, in fact, been abandoned in 1755. Even earlier the anti-Jewish sermons particularly frequent on the occasion of the Good Friday processions had been forbidden, putting an end to a habit lasting more than a century.

The preacher of the moment climbed onto a platform erected in front of the ghetto and from there launched the usual invectives against its inhabitants: "Perfidious Judeans, you were the ones who crucified and killed the Savior of the world", etc. In 1751 the government of the Jewish Nation of Florence petitioned the Secretary of the Royal Law, in charge of ecclesiastical affairs, who recognized the validity of their complaint. Two years later a similar pronouncement was made by the same Secretary about the problems arising from the diffusion of a rather badly written poem that was sung by scamps in the streets. Even from the title, "The Marriage of Baruccabà with the Gnora Luna, performed the 10th of September, in the time of the booths", showed its satirical intentions against the Jews. Its diffusion was prohibited, citing earlier proclamations, particularly the one of 1735, that prohibited molesting the Jews. These were small things, but they were indications of a change in the atmosphere.

More concrete measures were taken in 1778 when Peter Leopold established that Jews, too, could take part in the city councils (*comunitativi*, as they then called it) with the same rights as the others. It is true that the Jewish councilors could not be elected to the office of "Gonfaloniere" or "Priore" (today we would say, mayor and municipal magistrate). It is also true that election did not derive from a personal right, but from the nomination by the Community. It is no less true, however, that the presence of a Jew in the city council was an extraordinary fact for those times and for Florence. (In Livorno, on the other hand, such a right had been exercised since the community was founded).

The following year, the Grand Duke moved against a measure taken by the Academy of the *Faticanti* to exclude the Jews. Peter Leopold sustained the petition presented to him by the offended parties and from then on, no one contested the right of the Jews to belong to literary and scientific academies.

The spirit with which the sovereign faced the whole question is clearly evident from the answer he gave to a request coming from Pitigliano (a town in the area of Grosseto which was home to a small but flourishing Jewish community) asking to clarify exactly how the Jews were to be treated. The very simple answer was: "like all the other subjects of His Royal Highness." But it was not so in reality. The Jews continued to be excluded from the public administration, from the most important political offices, from the practice of law, etc. But they had at least started along the road that led to equality, so that when the French Revolution brought the gift of emancipation to the Tuscan Jews, it seemed more like the natural completion of a process which had already begun rather than an unforeseen and unthinkable novelty to be welcomed with manifestations of jubilation.

The sale of the ghetto directly to the Jews between 1779 and 1780, though due to external factors (the severe administrative disorder of the property and burden that its maintenance placed on the

State), had an evident and decisive importance in the process of the Florentine Jews' emancipation. Obvious advantages also came to them from the suppression of the Inquisition in 1782.

Still the Jews were far from being integrated into the social fabric. Popular hostility, deriving from centuries of anti-Jewish propaganda on the part of a large number of the Catholic clergy, remained intact. Anti-Leopoldian and anti-Jansenist riots in various Tuscan cities immediately after Peter Leopold's departure to became Emperor (1790) targeted the Jews as one of their main objects in Livorno and Florence. In the city of Livorno the insurrection of Santa Giulia left some Jews wounded and damaged the quarter in which they lived. On the 9th of June, 1790, in the capital of the Grand Duchy there were disorders which were calmed rather quickly thanks to the intervention of the city's archbishop, Antonio Martini and his vicar Agostino Albergotti. (The higher echelon of the ecclesiastical hierarchy was often less imbued with anti-Jewish sentiment than the lower clergy).

At this point the problems became intertwined with the tumultuous events of the French Revolution which soon affected Tuscany. Among both the Christians and the Jews, few realized the sense of this innovation, however, and often both entrenched themselves in conservative positions. A convention of Rabbis, held in Florence in 1796, dwelt only on the religious aspects, refusing every hypothesis of reform. In the end they confirmed the validity of the strictest orthodoxy.

The 25th of March, 1799, the French, who were the rulers of Florence, proclaimed the Jews' full equality with the Christians. Both became citizens with the same rights and without any distinctions. It was the so-called first Jewish emancipation. But once again, between the solemn pronouncement of a principle and its translation into reality a great distance remained. The *Jewish Nation* of Florence, as well as of the other localities in which a Jewish community was present, remained separated from the surrounding social context. The Jews themselves, unprepared for this new legal and social position, imposed on them from outside, were uncertain and hesitant. Not unreasonably, they were afraid that this gift would be precarious and would depend on the circumstances. What had been given could be taken away and cancelled. The French, who considered themselves liberators and expected gratitude from those they had helped, soon began to ask for tangible signs of thanks. On July 26th, 1799, they imposed a forced loan on the Florentine Jewish community. It was only the first of a series of such measures, destined to become a habit particularly during the Napoleonic period.

In the fifteen years that followed, there were continual rapid changes. In the summer of 1799 the French, who had been beaten in northern Italy, had to abandon Tuscany. Florence fell into the hands of *Sanfedist* [reactionary] bands, whose anti-Jewish feelings were basic to their beliefs. (In Siena thirteen Jews fell victim to a regular *pogrom*, while the Jews were banished forever from Monte San Savino, near Arezzo, etc.). But the next year, the victory at Marengo restored the French to a position of predominance in Italy, and the Grand Duchy was once again occupied by Napoleon. After including it in his political design, he handed the Duchy over to the House of Bourbon with the name of the State of Etruria. At the end of 1807 the last remaining pretense of autonomy was lost. Tuscany was annexed directly to France and subjected to its jurisdiction. It would remain that way until May of 1814, when the throne was restored to Grand Duke Ferdinand III of Lorraine after Napoleon's fall.

Obviously the Florentines and the Tuscans in general were subject to the blows and counter-blows, and the Jews even more so than the others. This was so because they were considered to be very close to the French, by whom they had been emancipated. (Therefore, they were considered by the common people to be Jacobins, enemies of the Christian religion, and rich besides). Popular resentment for the hardships borne in those years easily made them turn against the Jews every time an occasion arose. But out of prudence the Jews had been lukewarm supporters of both revolutionary and Napoleonic France. They received a citation of loyalty from Ferdinand III as soon as he reassumed the crown.

Bibliographical note

See my essays: *Gli ebrei in Toscana nel passaggio dal Granducato al Regno d'Etruria*, in *La Toscana e la Rivoluzione francese*, edited by Ivan Tognarini (Naples: Edizioni Scientifiche Italiane, 1994), pp. 475-498, and *1799: gli ebrei italiani nella bufera antigiacobina* (Florence: Giuntina, 1999).

THE RESTORATION: ECONOMIC RELATIONS

The Restoration essentially brought the Florentine and Tuscan Jews back to their previous situation under a moderate regime which was in certain ways even benevolent towards them. But it re-affirmed and intended to perpetuate the old inequality. The Jews could have some recognized privileges – as in the case of the Jews of Livorno – but no rights. All the Tuscans, from citizens went back to being subjects, and the Jews, placed under the protection of the sovereign, were doubly subjects. They were once again excluded from public employment, from military service, from the legal profession, and from important administrative positions. Mixed marriages were once again prohibited, as well as any sexual relations between anyone from the *Jewish Nation* and anyone from the Christian world. The only notable difference was that they were made equal to all the others as far as civil and penal law was concerned (except in cases involving matrimonial law which required special treatment). It was a step forward, and at the same time a step backward: forward because the measure followed the principle of the equality of all before the law, but a step backward because the Jews lost the autonomy that they had enjoyed earlier.

The seed, in any case, had been planted. It grew slowly and with difficulty, but in the end the Jews would be the leading actors in their second emancipation, which would turn out to be more solid and longer lasting than the first one. It would be interrupted only by Fascism's absurd racial laws.

During the time coinciding with the last period of the Lorraine rule (1814-1859), while Florence grew from around 80,000 inhabitants to around 130-140,000 on the eve of Italian unification, the Jews increased proportionately (from about 1,200 they grew to about 2,000). However, their influence on city life was strongly felt as can be seen from research done by scholars dealing with that period (particularly, Fabio Bertini and Romano Paolo Coppini, who are interested in the financial activities of the first half of the 1800's in Tuscany).

Starting in the period of Leopold's reign, the Jews acquired the right they did not have earlier (except in Livorno and Pitigliano) of owning and selling real estate, both houses and land. It was no little concession, and the Jews immediately took advantage of it. They moved from one town to another, occupying important positions in every type of business. They went to live outside the ghetto (in Florence one of their favorite places was Via Larga – today Via Cavour, one of the most important streets in the city). They did business with bankers, with the most prominent men, and with the authorities of the non-Jewish world. At that level the difference in religious faith did not inhibit or separate them as it did at the lower levels of society. Money is a great equalizer.

The case of Servadio (or Servaddio) Servi and his sons David and Samuel was typical. The father tried his fortune in 1788, moving (almost certainly from Pitigliano) to the capital with his numerous, but poor family. His son Samuel's fortunate marriage allowed him to use the bride's dowry to set up a business selling fabrics with the help of his other son, David, who in turn married the daughter of Cesare Lampronti, a banker from Ferrara. The marriage allowed Servadio to overcome a serious economic crisis at the end of the century. At the beginning of the 1800's during the French period, the three Servis, at first in partnership and later individually, went from commerce to banking, establishing relations with the bankers Fermi and Mondolfi and acquiring several farms.

Even more interesting was the case of Angiolo Finzi, who was the owner of one building in the ghetto in 1782, but shortly after became the owner of the whole ghetto – and then of the old and new ghettos – in various stages (in 1789, in 1815, in 1817, and in 1818).

At any rate, among the Finzis, the most important figure was, without a doubt, the banker Raffaello. A prominent member of the Freemasons, he was "one of the richest storekeepers in Florence, who had interest in a whole series of large and small firms, demonstrating a great versatility in business" (as Bertini wrote). It is known that he speculated on the bankruptcy of the Dini and

Guadagni families (together with the Jews Levi Mortera and David Luzzatti, the Florentine banker Emanuele Fenzi and Vincenzio Danty of Livorno) and on public debt. He bought villas and farms, founded partnerships to buy shops, and formed groups to finance important building firms (for example the one established with Gino Capponi and Cosimo Ridolfi between 1831 and 1834, to construct two bridges on the Arno), etc.

Though not comparable with Raffaello Finzi's wealth, Cesare Lampronti, doctor and banker, had a very prominent position, not only from a financial point of view, but also for his social prestige. Arriving in Livorno from Ferrara, where he was born in 1755, he then moved to Florence where he held the office of Chancellor of the *Jewish Nation* from at least 1790. In 1801-2, at the beginning of the French period, he was among those who were owed money by the Florentine *Community* (today we would call it the city government). In the Napoleonic years he was involved in a considerable exchange of promissory notes, together with Ezechia Baraffael (his father-in-law) and Marquis Carlo Gerini, who organized the deal following the bankruptcy of the Della Tosa family. He formed a partnership with the bankers Jacopo Tartini Salvatici and Girolamo Severi in order to buy large tracts of land south of Livorno and was owed large amounts of money by a well-known businessman, Spinello Spinelli. In 1814 he was councilor of the *camera comunitativa* and in the following year member of the general and central deputation for military provisions. In 1816 he was the deputy for family taxes, while he was simultaneously busy with a plan for a mixed administration in the iron industry, financing the mines on the Island of Elba. In 1817 he, too, appears as one of the owners of the ghetto and in 1818 he was the president of the Chamber of Commerce (after being a judge in the corresponding court). After 1820 his bank, *Lampronti & C.,* was considered one of the most solid, capable of engaging numerous activities. In 1826 it obtained the tobacco concession, a sector that in Tuscany was traditionally entrusted to the Jews. Perfectly integrated into the society in which he lived, respected and esteemed by the authorities, indistinguishable from any other businessman whatever his religious faith, Lampronti did not shirk the job of representing the *Nation* to which he belonged. Even in 1824, when he was already quite old, documents illustrate his activities to safeguard the interests and rights not only of the Florentine Jews, but also of Jews living in other parts of Tuscany who turned to him for advice and assistance. For all his contemporaries he was seen as a charismatic leader.

Also notable were the two Orvieto brothers, Abramo and Isacco, who during the Napoleonic period bought farms, lent money and in general took part in banking activities. They formed a partnership with both Christian and Jewish bankers and financiers to acquire stores. Then there were Leon Vita Levi who speculated on the sale of national goods; Leon Vita Luzzatti (from Rovigo and a Freemason) who dealt in grain and moneylending; Elia Coen and Daniele Pegna, whose business after an initial period of prosperity then declined, etc. As Bertini rightly noted, "the tax paid by each family to the community gives us an idea of who were the wealthiest. Leon Vita Finzi paid 1680 lire in 1811, Elia Usigli, Leon's father, 1600, Salomone Della Vida 700, Ambron 700, followed by Mondolfi, Lampronti and others".

For the period of the Restoration we unfortunately do not have studies such as the one conducted with great precision by Fabio Bertini (which we have amply used) for the Napoleonic Age, but some studies (especially Coppini's) on the economic characteristics of that period show that the participation of the Jews in business and finance did not cease although it underwent no slight modification to adapt itself to the times. Speculative activities typical of the Napoleonic period, stimulated by the requisition of ecclesiastical goods and by the sale of state properties, developed in such a way that one could see a relatively new bourgeois class emerge and mix with the Florentine nobility which traditionally engaged in business. Numerous Jews took part in these activities, with no noticeable differences between them and the others. Acquisitions of land, buildings and stores, financial and credit speculation, commercial transactions, division of the estates of bankrupt families, etc. show all businessmen active in the same way: Jews and Christians associated in the same firms, societies and banks. Moneylending − traditionally considered typical of the Jews − no longer belonged to them any more than it did to the non-Jews.

The census of 1841, showing the presence of 1,543 Jews in Florence, also gives us some clues about their social and economic conditions. It is difficult, however, to compare them with what we know about the Jews of Livorno. The criteria assigned for the survey were very elastic and in some cases even subjective.

For example the work categories differed according to the discretion of the compiler and varied from place to place. Who were, for example, the almost one hundred *industrianti* found in Florence? Were they people who made a living in some way (mainly as traveling notions salesmen), as we tend to believe, or were they unqualified manual workers, *operanti,* as they were called then, and as they were called in other lists? What is the "tutor and caretaker of one's own children", that we find in Siena (and nowhere else)? And how is a *attendente a casa* [housewife] characterized? What is the "capitalist" that we find in Pisa and how is he different from a banker, also named? Etc.

While taking these difficulties into account and using caution, we can still find some useful data. The housewives in Florence were 200: slightly less than 13% of the total Jewish population (and 25.5% of the women). It is the lowest percentage of all the Tuscan communities (respectively 26.7% and 54% in Siena; 23.3% and 45.6% in Pisa; 19.9% and 39% in Livorno, as we have already seen, and 18% and 35.5% in Pitigliano). Were the Jewish women more active in Florence than elsewhere? If that is the case, does it denote their relative emancipation derived from living in the capital?

There were 14 bankers belonging to nine different families (Ambron, Curiel, Della Ripa, Galligo, Gentilomo, Lampronti, Modigliani, Mondolfi, Senigaglia), but one has the impression that some names are missing. The Finzi, for example, appear only among the thirty "property owners". Two "property owners and discount brokers", and six "discount brokers" must be added to the list.

Fully 65 families out of 309 (21%) lived outside the ghetto, though many of them had houses on the streets adjacent to it. But the Finzi, the Mondolfi, and the doctor Giuseppe Levi resided on Via Larga; the Castelli on Via Martelli; the Dina in Piazza del Duomo; the Gentilomo on the Lungarno; etc. There was even a family – the Viterbo – that lived outside the S. Miniato Gate. 141 families (almost half) lived in the New Ghetto (and we deduce that the remaining 30%, though it is not said explicitly, lived in the Old Ghetto).

The richest family seems to be that of Raffaello Finzi Morelli, made up of six people including him. It employed one Jewish governess and seven Christian servants (3 maids, 2 waiters, 1 cook and 1 assistant cook). Families that lived in similar conditions were those of Doctor Giacomo Almansi, Alessandro Ambron, Giuseppe Ambron, Giuseppe Della Ripa, Abram David Ferni, David Franchetti, Lodovico Mondolfi, and Graziano Senigaglia.

Besides the bankers, discount brokers, etc., about fifty other people were connected to the business world (9 bank ministers, 23 bank attendants, 10 moneychangers and exchange brokers, 3 discount mediators, etc.). More than 150 Jews were active in commerce (76 shopkeepers, 60 shop attendants, 8 jewelry brokers, 6 book sellers, etc.). To these must be added, at the lowest step of the ladder, around 100 *industrianti*, as we have already said. The two who had a notions shop were mentioned separately. Manufacturing involved five or six people as entrepreneurs (1 rag paper maker, 2 silk manufacturers, 1 inspector of plumes, 1 eyeglass manufacturer, etc.), plus 50 other product brokers who could be considered part of the commercial sector.

Then there were a number of other occupations. The Florentine Jews were everything from apprentice silversmiths to midwives, from grocers to furriers, from designers to poultry sellers, from architects to porters, etc.; one or two people per category. But the most numerous were those who offered services, such as domestic servants, waiters, cooks, etc., in all about 80. About 15 people were employed as teachers, in various ways and at various levels (5 elementary teachers, 8 Hebrew language teachers, 1 calligraphy teacher, 2 school directors). The students (of painting, music, medicine, and pharmacy) were 8. Printers, as we have already seen, were six.

The necessarily indigent (the poor with no hope of bettering themselves) were 24. But this number, like all those that we find for this category, is not to be trusted since the evaluation was entirely up to the census taker, and the criteria varied greatly from one to the other.

In Florence (and in Tuscany in general) for over forty years the land transfers and financial speculation typical of the chaotic Napoleonic years were no longer possible, at least not on the same scale. They appeared once again, for obvious reasons, in 1859 and in the following years we can find further confirmation of what we have already written.

In the *Toscanina* [little Tuscany] of the end of the Lorraine period, everything was quieter and hidden. But it is necessary to note that around 1830 more vivacious business initiatives began to be evident.

Bibliographical note

See: Fabio BERTINI, *Nobiltà e finanza tra '700 e '800. Debito e affari a Firenze nell'età napoleonica* (Florence: Centro Editoriale Toscano, 1989); Romano Paolo COPPINI, "Ceti dirigenti e banche nel periodo della Restaurazione", in *I Lorena in Toscana*, edited by Zeffiro Ciuffoletti and Leonardo Rombai (Florence: Olschki, 1989); Romano Paolo COPPINI, "Banche e speculazioni a Firenze nel primo ventennio unitario", in *Quaderni storici*, n. 32, XI, fasc. II (May-August 1976); Mirella SCARDOZZI, "Per l'analisi del ceto commerciale fiorentino nella prima metà dell'Ottocento: i setaioli", in *Quaderni storici*, n. 70, XXIV, fasc. I (April 1989), pp. 235-268.

PARTICIPATION IN THE *RISORGIMENTO*

The most valid way for the Jews to reach full emancipation was by participating in the *Risorgimento* [Italian unification]. At least two considerations spurred them in that direction: first, the fact that Italy's political unification was being forged by liberal and democratic movements could only help their cause, and second, the fact that most of the Jews naturally belonged to the middle class induced them to collaborate with the bourgeoisie leading those movements. The minute the Jews stopped being subjects and guests of this or that state in the Italian peninsula, they become Italian Jews and, even more, Jewish Italians. The noun "Italian" made them similar in rights to everyone else. The adjective "Jewish" was merely a cultural characteristic that, though distinguishable, could easily be accommodated just like so many others within the new nation.

Such an important transformation did not take place without risks, the most serious being the loss of their traditional physiognomy. The Jew who stopped being different and was not obliged to act differently day after day could not avoid feeling contrasting sentiments of euphoria and confusion, somewhat like what happens when you come into the light after being in the dark for a long time. From then on the problem of the Italian Jews (or of the Jewish Italians) was to maintain their distinctive identity without losing any of their newly gained equality. It was a problem common to all the minorities, to be sure, but for the Jews it was even more urgent considering the richness and uniqueness of their history, which unlike others was so closely tied to their rites and to a very pervasive religion with its very distinctive and minutely defined character. Becoming Italian, or *more* Italian, at times meant becoming *less* Jewish, and that, as we know, is what happened to many people. A current of secularization touched everyone in the second half of the 1800's and mixed Jews together with non-Jews. The only ones to resist on both sides were those whom we would call fundamentalists today: for example, on one hand there were the Rabbis who strenuously defended orthodoxy, and, on the other, separated from them by an unbridgeable abyss and reciprocal adversity were the Jesuits. They shared, however, an aversion to religious indifference and, even more, to skepticism, irreverence, and atheism. These were seen as the collapse of the great moral barrier that had been erected by religion (or religions) over a long period of time to preside over a society that was just because it was blessed by God and blessed by God because it was just.

The minority, in short, ran the risk of being dissolved in the majority. In Italy – but not only in Italy – integration was a prelude to assimilation. Time worked in favor of homogenization. It was easy to identify the Jew as long as you made him wear a yellow badge or closed him in a ghetto. When he came out, he mixed with the others and was hidden. Already in the second generation he could be indistinguishable from the majority not only for others, but also for himself. The Jew, when he became a patriot, willingly forgot that for centuries he had been unfailingly considered a member of another *Nation.* Later, from beyond the Alps, anti-semitism arrived to remind him of it, so that the monster of religious prejudice was supplanted by the even more fearful and perverse monster of secular prejudice, bristling with biological and racial sophisms like poisonous thorns. The Jew was obliged to recover his identity, whether he wanted to or not, and to take a step backward into the past. He responded by once again declaring his fidelity to his *Nation* through Zionism.

The divisions and wavering over Zionism, typical of the Italian Jews at the end of the 19th and the beginning of the 20th centuries were fully understandable. The Jews living in the Italian peninsula were truly on the Island of Divine Dew, as the name *Italia* could be translated into Hebrew according to a fanciful etymology. Here the fierce anti-semitism raging in Central and Eastern Europe did not bear down with all its oppressive weight. There were no *pogroms* in Italy and the chronicles of the Dreyfus affair did not provoke anything more than some uneasiness. It was not by chance that the *Protocols of the Elders of Zion* were not published by Giovanni Preziosi until 1921. Most of the Jews living in Italy sincerely professed their loyalty to what they considered their first and true homeland – Italy – and consequently attributed to Zionism an ethical value of human solidarity, rather than a political one.

These developments in the Jewish condition, with their problems and contradictions, were certainly not foreseeable in the first half of the 1800's. And yet the first seeds, the first indications were already there at the time of the Restoration, when the Jews entered the Masonic Lodges, the secret societies, and then the *Giovine Italia.* They were present on the battlegrounds of the wars of independence, fighting for the Italian cause and their own emancipation at the same time. As an appeal directed specifically at the Tuscan Jews written by an anonymous Catholic friend, with all the rhetorical emphasis common in those times, said:

> For you, Italian Israelites, Italy is no longer just a place of refuge that your ancestors' bad fortune caused you to discover. It is your native terrain, it is your new homeland. Now that you have been admitted to the national banquet, you may call it that.

The contribution made by the Tuscan Jews to the cause of the *Risorgimento* had no particularly unique characteristics. It was obviously connected to that of the Jews in the other Italian states. Moreover, the Jews' contribution blended more and more with the actions of other patriots of various political tendencies regardless of religious distinctions; this fact was already, per se, evidence of a conquest and a mature conscience. The nature of Jewish participation cannot be singled out, but it did reinforce whatever it was that made a person join and show solidarity to the cause. A similar phenomenon reappeared much later with those Jews that entered the Resistance Movement. It was, naturally, the choice of only a few: not only because the Jews were a minority, but mainly because the *Risorgimento* movement was essentially elitist.

The most lively and politically active center in Tuscany (as Salvatore Foà, the most important scholar of the Jewish presence in the *Risorgimento* has noted) was Livorno, called by Metternich "the workshop of the revolution". Here, in 1814, the police discovered the most important Masonic lodge in Tuscany: the St. Jean d'Ecosse or Napoleone, founded at the beginning of 1808. Various Jews belonged to it: Isach and Giovanni Grant (English nationals), Moisè and Abram Busnach, Moisè Coen Bacri, Daniel Moisè, Jacob Recanati, all defined as storekeepers, and Isach Altias, defined as proprietor. Almost contemporarily the *Buongoverno* discovered two other Masonic lodges in Florence: one named after Napoleon (founded on the 25th of December, 1807) and the other after his sister Elisa (founded on the 21st of July, 1809) but united with the other lodge in 1813 when it was about to be disbanded. In both, next to names from the Florentine nobility, one found names of Jews: Felice Coen and his uncle Angelo, Giuseppe Luzzati, Graziadio Finzi and a certain Fermi. Many were followers of Marquis Pietro Torrigiani, considered by the *Buongoverno* "one of the first Masons, firmly faithful to Napoleon and *cicisbeo* of the little Jewess, the wife of Raffaello Finzi". The police rarely missed a chance to add to the political information a negative note on the accused person's habits or morals.

In 1815 a commission composed of Ranieri Fortunato Benvenuti, Luigi Cremani and Giovanni Fini was established to investigate those who had distinguished themselves as *partitanti francesi* [pro-French partisans] during the Napoleonic period. Cremani had already become sadly famous for condemning hundreds of Tuscan Jacobins in 1799. Numerous punishments emanated from the commission and several struck Jews.

Another Masonic lodge was discovered in 1817. It was called *San Giovanni e San Paolo dell'Oriente di Livorno* [St. John and St. Paul of the Orient of Livorno] and was connected to a parish in a suburb of Livorno called San Martino in Salviano.

At least a part of the Masonic lodges – the most radical ones – gave rise to *Carboneria* lodges [secret political societies] in which many Jews were also members. The Jews of Livorno, active in trade and commerce everywhere, were in a particularly favorable position to establish politically significant contacts abroad and to bring prohibited printed material into Tuscany. It seems that the first *Carboneria* organization arose in Livorno in September of 1818. In any case it spread rapidly. At the end of 1819, according to Giuseppe Valtancoli, who acted as a police spy within the secret societies and was never discovered, in Livorno alone there were two hundred members, of whom forty were permanent associates. Valtancoli himself in one of his messages to the *Buongoverno* wrote: "It may be observed that the *Carboneria* has spread mainly within the *Jewish Nation*. Jewish ignorance and cruelty have willingly fostered the knowledge of the absurd immorality of the first degree which was more easily explained than the Masons' symbolic degrees. The Jews of Livorno have carried it to Florence." Here too, we note the tendency of police associates to morally denigrate their political adversaries. Valtancoli – who liked to give himself Jewish aliases and called himself Isach during his spying activity – earlier had affirmed: "The *Carboneria* was known for its small secret meetings whose scope was debauchery, and they all ended in drunkenness and in whore houses." Often the police, even when it knew the names of the conspirators or at least had well-grounded suspicions about them, abstained from intervention because to strike them would mean putting trade at a great risk. Economic concerns reined in political ones.

In the following period activities that aimed at changing the order of things in Tuscany assumed two forms: one conspiratorial and one openly moderate-liberal. The latter had the *Gabinetto Vieusseux* of Florence and its magazine *Antologia* as its main reference points. In both cases we still find names of Jews. In Livorno members of the secret society of the *Veri Italiani* [True Italians] inspired by Buonarroti, included the Jews Emanuele Montefiore, Angelo Ottolenghi, Beniamino Coen, Angelo della Torre, Levi Benfasson, Felice Calvo, and Samuele Morais. Among all of them Morais, a butcher called *Baulino*, was the "bloodiest and most characteristic". In Florence they entered the innovative cultural movement whose adherents included Gino Capponi, Cosimo Ridolfi, Raffaello Lambruschini, etc., and also Doctor Emanuele Basevi (who became part of the legislative assembly in 1849) as well as the Uzielli brothers. As Foà wrote: "The *Antologia* (January, 1830) had the courage to publish an article by Gabriello Pepe in favor of the Jews" and when the *Antologia* was suppressed [1833] and *bulletins* were published against police orders, two Jews, a certain Ludovico Mondolfi and Abramo Philippson, were arrested for having affixed those writings."

Gina Formiggini wrote about the figure of Mondolfi. Originally from Ancona, he lived in Florence from 1824, where his father, Sabato, was a well-known banker and *Chargé des Affaires du Trésor* during the Napoleonic period. After belonging to the *Carboneria*, he had joined the *Giovine Italia* and was given the job of calming down Guerrazzi, whose imprudence attracted the attention of the police. Mondolfi was arrested and put into the Florentine prison of the Murate but was advised that the imprisonment could be commuted into exile. He accepted exile and continued his activity as an agitator in Bologna, Modena, Paris and London. There he was in close contact with Mazzini whose stay abroad he helped to finance. He then went through a political crisis and changed to a moderate-liberal position. Influenced by Gino Capponi he was involved in the schools of mutual tuition (which were one of the objectives of Florentine cultural circles in their quest for renewal). Then he made friends abroad with Terenzio Mamiani. After returning to Italy in 1835, his finance company went bankrupt in 1848. He died in Livorno in 1874, almost a pauper. Alessandro Franchetti, who was born in Livorno in 1809 and died in Florence in 1874, had a somewhat similar story. A well-known and generous philanthropist, he had a profound knowledge of law, but could not practice that profession because he was a Jew. He studied literature and history, founding the *Biblioteca Dantesca* [the Dante Library]. As a young man he, too, was influenced by Mazzini's ideas, and, like so many others, he later assumed a less revolutionary political orientation, participating in the movement for educational renewal in Tuscany.

In 1832 some Florentine liberals, including a certain Fermo, son of a Jewish banker, made a feeble attempt to unite Italy in a constitutional government that was to have Count Alessandro Colonna Walewski, Napoleon's illegitimate son, as its head. In the meantime the D'Ancona family, coming from Pesaro, took refuge in Pisa to escape the persecutions aimed at the Jews during Leone XII's pontificate. Among them two brothers, Sansone and Alessandro D'Ancona, distinguished themselves in cultural and political activities, making their house a meeting place for patriots and giving hospitality to Luigi Carlo Farini, among others. Also in those years secret political activities continued in Livorno, where Franchetti and Montreal were busy with charitable work and social assistance for the city government and the entire population.

Relations between Piedmont and Tuscany were obviously spontaneous and natural within the framework of the *Risorgimento* movements, but they took on a particular meaning for the Jews. Up to the concession of the 1848 Statute, in fact, the condition of Piedmont Jews had been one of the worst, along with their brothers who lived in the Papal States. The milder conditions in Tuscany made it a land suitable for spreading propaganda for Jewish emancipation (and even David Levi dedicated himself to it.) In the *biennio riformista* [two years of reform] the Florentine newspapers *Il Sabatino* and *Alba*, which had democratic tendencies, and *Patria*, a moderate paper, conducted a campaign in this direction. In Pisa *L'Italia,* a paper distributed mainly in Livorno and edited by Giuseppe Montanelli, at that time close to Neoguelf positions, did likewise. Another Piedmontese Jew, Salvatore Debenedetti from Novara, after years of passionately supporting Mazzini, wrote for the *Corriere Livornese*, and for a while, he edited it. Like him, the Livorno Jew Mario Consigli, who professed democratic and republican beliefs, wrote in *Eco della sera* (to which Debenedetti also contributed) and edited *Il Calambrone* and *L'Italia Repubblicana*.

Prepared by this climate, between the 7th and 8th of September 1847, a two-day meeting of Jewish-Christian friendship was held in Livorno's Piazza San Leopoldo, in the presence of a numerous public. Among the speakers was Rabbi Elia Benamozegh, who exhorted his fellow Jews to love Italy, after God, above every other worldly affection, and David Busnach, nicknamed Ciuci, who had a secular outlook and was elected to the extraordinary junta in April, 1849.

These activities were not without impact even on the Grand Duke's policy. Leopold II, between 1845 and 1846, was induced to take measures to align the rights of the Jews of Livorno more and more with those of his other subjects, and at last, with the concession of the Statute of February 11, 1848, all discrimination against the Jews was eliminated.

This liberating action was not as sudden as it may appear at first. It was the result of a petition sent to the Grand Duke on November 2, 1847, by a commission organized by the Jewish communities of Tuscany asking for full Israelite emancipation. Moreover, it had been preceded by a rather lively debate that spread throughout all of Italy although it had its main headquarters in Piedmont. One of the main protagonists was, without a doubt, Massimo d'Azeglio with his *On the civil emancipation of the Israelites*, published, not by chance, in Florence by the Le Monnier publishing house in 1848.

On the 6th of May, 1852, however, Leopold II signed a decree to abolish the Statute. The Jews returned to their former condition.

They had enjoyed full civil and political rights for four years, but the brevity of it did not make the step backward any less bitter. In the space of two generations they had enjoyed two periods of liberty: the first time when Tuscany was under French domination between 1808 and 1814 (aside from a preview in Livorno from 1796 and in 1799), and now in connection with the revolutionary events of 1848. The suppression of the Statute unexpectedly and unjustly *imprisoned* them again. The Tuscan Jewish world, which had been so loyalist up to that point, so ready to recognize the merits of the reigning dynasty beginning with Peter Leopold, and so quick to put themselves under the Lorraines' protection, at the first news of what was in the offing this time dared to intervene and to make its voice heard by the sovereign, though only by means of petitions. On April 1st of 1852 the representative of the *Università israelitica* [Jewish community] of Livorno took the initiative, and then on April 6th it was the turn of the *Università israelitica* of Florence, of Pisa and of Siena (evidently in agreement among themselves). Pitigliano was not included in the list, but just a week later, on the 13th of April, Jacob Lampronti, secretary of the Florentine community, and the lawyer Vincenzo Landrini repeated the appeal to the sovereign in the name of all five of the Tuscan *Università israelitiche*.

They received no answer. The Grand Duke firmly upheld his decision, which was in line with his policy's reactionary turn, destined to alienate every residual sympathy on the part of the Tuscan population. Having returned to the throne thanks to the Austrian army that he himself had called in (and that perpetrated a true massacre in Livorno), Leopold II had progressively abandoned the liberalizing legislation of his ancestor Peter Leopold. He reinstated the death penalty and signed a concordat with the Vatican (April 30, 1851) that was a true negation of the Grand Duchy's jurisdictional tradition.

At the origin of the Grand Duke's resolution about the Jews was the fact that he wanted to establish closer ties to the Vatican. The question was examined and discussed by the Lorraine government for three whole months, between the beginning of February and the beginning of May, 1852. Although all agreed that the statute should be abolished, opinions differed concerning the fate of the Jews and other non-Catholics. The majority of the ministers and functionaries – Giovanni Baldasseroni, Leonida Landucci, Vincenzo di Casigliano, Niccolò Lami, Giovanni Bologna – was for the continuation of the rights already granted, while a minority – Antonio Bicchierai, Cesare Boccella and Scipione Bargagli – was for a return to the earlier condition. The debate was opened with a report by Bicchierai in which the right of the Jews to practice law was the main object of contention. At most the Jews could be allowed to practice medicine and, in the legal field, only the professions that excluded any contact with canon law. Morality, according to Bicchierai, was founded on religion (and, naturally, the true religion was Catholicism). Shortly after Boccella sent a memo on the question of the Jews to the Grand Duke: according to him it could not be solved except in agreement with the Pope, or at least, with his approval. Marquis Scipione Bargagli, Minister of Tuscany at the Holy See and, as such, in direct contact with Cardinal Antonelli and Pius IX himself, confirmed the following: that the secretary of State and the Pope were favorable to both the abolition of the Statute and a limitation of the Jews' rights. These measures seemed to them completely coherent with the concordat signed the year before. "The fears of a reaction of the Israelite Nation and of Tuscan public opinion" were to be considered "exaggerated", continued the Marquis, whose opinion was destined to prevail.

The debate was not kept so secret that news of it could not filter out. On March 31st, 1852, the Royal procurator of Livorno, Isolani, informed the Minister of Justice and Pardon that the Jews of the city, who had had news of the imminent abolition of the Statute, seemed very worried. Doctor Nissim, he added, had expressed these fears: "A restoration of the old restrictions would offend many newly acquired positions and many legitimate hopes." As we have seen, in the days following April 1st, the various Jewish Communities of Tuscany sent a request to the Grand Duke to give up his plans. On April 20th, the newspaper *Il Costituzionale* spoke of rumors that the Jews would be restored to their earlier condition, thanks to requests coming from the Vatican. It protested with vigor and threatened: "If the measure proposed against the Jews is adopted, the rich Jewish banking houses of Florence and Livorno will probably take their immense riches away to Piedmont, where religious tolerance and liberty still exist."

On their part, on March 18, 1852, Baldasseroni and the others wrote an historic memo in which interesting information appeared.

First of all, the number of Jews then resident in Tuscany was estimated to be 7,500, and then there was a discussion of which university degrees would be available to the Jews. As for the degree in medicine, it is known that Jews had always had access to it. A sovereign resolution of May 20, 1836, also confirmed the Jews' full right to exercise the medical profession. Between 1815 and 1851, 124 Jews had graduated in medicine in Pisa, while Siena had graduated 33 Jews and other non-Catholics. In that same period 36 Jews had enrolled in medicine, 19 in surgery, and 9 in pharmacy in the Medical College of Florence (and they added, "of these some treat true Christian families").

The question of degrees in law was more complex. Since in Pisa it was only possible to earn a degree *in utroque jure* (that is, in civil law and canon law at the same time), the Jews were excluded for a long time except during the period of French occupation, 1808-1814, when no limitation was imposed on them. Even if the report did not state it explicitly, it seemed that, from 1820, Jews were permitted to earn a degree only in civil law, a privilege extended to all the *heterodox* students with the education reform of June 2, 1841. In fact it pointed out immediately afterward that "from 1820 through 1851, 231 Jewish and Heterodox students earned a degree in Pisa, while another 53 earned the same degree at the University of Siena". In the years that the statute was valid, five Jews were admitted to the legal profession. It adds that since the beginning of a commercial court in Florence (between 1814 and 1839) some Jewish storekeepers had participated as judges to the satisfaction of all. The exclusion of the Jews from the legal profession, it deduces, would be unjust, hateful, and politically inopportune. Also noted was the fact that, in the current year of 1852, 38 young Jews and non-Catholics were enrolled in physical science and mathematics in Pisa, and 18 in law in Siena. The report concluded, finally, by underlining the loyalty of the Jews to the reigning house (except for some unrest and turbulence in 1796 and 1799, because of the evil influences of the French Revolution) and by expressing the hope that the abolition of the Statute would not be followed by the elimination of political rights already conceded. The only tangible result of this intervention was that Jews with law degrees were allowed to exercise their profession, but only in cases between Jews.

The Grand Duke, bound by political ties with Austria and no less rigid religious ties with the Pope, that he could not ignore, chose an intransigent policy. Because of that, full emancipation, destined to last for all the Italian Jews until the Fascist racial laws of 1938, arrived for the Tuscan Jews only after the unification of Italy, which was achieved by the wars of independence and the deeds of the *Mille* [Garibaldi's 1000 "red shirts"], in which the Tuscan Jews who participated were indistinguishable from the other Italians. Of the three possible ways of acquiring equal rights – accumulating wealth, converting to Christianity, or becoming Italians like all the others – the last was the most convincing.

Bibliographical note

For the participation of the Florentine and Tuscan Jews in the *Risorgimento*: Anna BARETTA, *Le società segrete in Toscana nel 1° decennio dopo la Restaurazione: 1814-1824* (Bologna: Forni, 1978); Salvatore FOÀ, *Gli ebrei nel Risorgimento italiano* (Rom: Carucci, 1978); Bruno DI PORTO, "L'approdo al crogiuolo risorgimentale", in *Rassegna Mensile di Israel*, L, 9-12 (Sept.-Dec. 1984), pp. 803-862; Gina FORMIGGINI, *Stella d'Italia, Stella di David. Gli ebrei dal Risorgimento alla Resistenza* (Milan: Mursia, 1970); and, naturally, my aforementioned essay *Gli ebrei toscani nell'età della Restaurazione.*

EDUCATION AND AID SOCIETIES

The activities undertaken by the Tuscan Jewish Communities in the fields of welfare and education were comparatively more numerous and intense than those of the surrounding society. Above all their attention to schools and education in general was very far from the indifference shown by civil and ecclesiastical authorities. As a matter of fact, the latter were often suspicious of attempts on the part of generally moderate-liberal elements from 1830 on to increase literacy and school attendance. Illiteracy and ignorance among the lower classes was the rule in a predominantly peasant society, and naturally not even the Jews – who were not peasants and whose religious tradition encouraged culture – were exempt from the prevailing conditions, but they were subject to these plagues to much lesser degree than the others.

To have a general picture of the situation it is necessary to refer to the 19th century as both an arrival point and as a starting point for the development of education and welfare activities. The 1841 census gave very useful indications on education. The compiler had to indicate, on that occasion, whether the person knew how to read and write, only read, or whether he was illiterate. It is clear that in the results obtained, there was a certain amount of subjectivity in the census official's evaluation, though we cannot say how much. If we assume that about 10% of the illiterates were pre-schoolers and we subtract them from the total, for the individual Jewish communities we get these percentages (in the following order: literates, semi-illiterates, illiterates) – in Livorno: 57%, 8%, 35%; in Florence: 68.5%, 5%, 26.5%; in Pisa: 74%, 6%, 20%; in Siena: 77%, no indication, 23%; in Pitigliano: 66%, 7%, 27%. When we recall that in Tuscany the general average sum of literates and semi-illiterates

was 19% (45.5% in Pisa; 45.1% in Florence), we can immediately
see the size of the phenomenon. Greater culture favors a higher socio-economic position and, vice versa, a higher socio-economic position favors higher culture.

It is also obvious that the more attention paid to the problem,
the greater the resources employed. Therefore, the *Università* of
Livorno and, partially, of Florence, were conspicuous compared to
the others, but not even the smaller communities – Siena or even
Pitigliano – lacked a spirit of organization. The autonomous character of these initiatives must be underlined: the subsidies came entirely from private donations, mainly in the form of bequests. As is
known, at that time the State (not only in Tuscany) in all of its
forms and at all levels from the central government to the peripheral
administrations was almost completely absent from the fields of
both social services and education. No public schools existed, no
academic degrees were required for teachers, no attention was paid
to school buildings, etc. The administrations of the individual Jewish communities made up for this lack. The government limited itself to approving the statutes of the various institutions, and the
Grand Duke, at times, praised the results.

For Livorno it is enough to say that in 1844 there were 18 different Jewish educational institutions: 13 for boys and 5 for girls.
They were divided into nursery schools, schools of mutual tuition, 4
religious high schools and 6 civil high schools. For girls there was a
nursery, a school of the first and second levels, a religious school,
and a school for pressers and seamstresses. The difference between
boys and girls is striking, not only for the quantity of schools, but
also and above all in comparison with what the surrounding non-
Jewish society offered in the way of education, which, as we have
already said, was incredibly lacking.

In Florence the attention given to education by the *Università
Israelitica* was probably even greater and dated from the 16th century, when, according to the history of charitable institutions written
by Passerini, a free elementary school was established for Jewish
children. Around the middle of the 19th century the school held
more than thirty youngsters between 7 and 16 years old. Placed under the care of the head Rabbi, it employed five teachers for five
classes, of which three were for Hebrew and two for profane subjects. But even more noteworthy was the nursery school, whose ori-

gins went all the way back to 1735, when an association was formed – the Tree of Life (*Etz Haim*), which still existed in the middle of the 1800's – with the goal of creating a nursery school for children under seven years of age and preparing them for religious education. (The first Jewish nursery school in Livorno was established in 1771). If we keep in mind that the first Italian nursery schools, inspired by Ferrante Aporti, began only in 1829, and that this type of scholastic organism arose in Florence only in 1834, we are necessarily impressed by the educational zeal typical of the Jewish communities. In 1835 the Florentine *Asilo Israelitico* [Jewish nursery school] that contained children from three to seven years of age (later the upper limit was changed to six years of age) reopened after a long period in which it had been closed. It underwent a series of reforms to make it similar to the other nursery schools of Florence, and less bound to religious instruction, which remained predominant in any case. Shortly after 1850 it contained forty children, both girls and boys, who ate there and dressed all alike in clothes that were donated to them.

For the Jews who were well-off there were private schools. Among these were the Salomone Fiorentino Institute for boys and the Salomone Sezzi Institute for girls.

In 1843 a school for young girls was founded to prepare them for the arts and trades. Forty girls between the ages of seven and fifteen attended, learning elements of Hebrew and Italian as well as female work. This school was the result of an initiative taken in 1825 by a Philanthropic Society of Arts and Trades, established by about 45 wealthy Florentine Jews (including names of Finzi, Fano, Baraffael, etc.) for the benefit of indigent people. The society announced its goals: "To subsidize the young people who want to apply themselves to the arts, encourage them in their careers, help them to find the means to feed their families, reconciling industriousness and honor." It met such strong resistance from the *massari* of the *Jewish Nation* that it was necessary for government officials and then the Grand Duke himself to intervene. The directors of the *Università* expressed two preoccupations. The first concerned the lower limit of 10 years of age (the upper was 16) appearing in the proposed by-laws for learning an artisan's trade in non-Jewish owned workshops and factories. For these youngsters they explicitly expressed a fear of "leaving them abandoned to their Catholic teachers at too tender an age (in spite of their unceasing surveillance) to be able to defend themselves from the temptations offered them". The lower age limit, therefore, had to be changed to thirteen years of age. This fear increased when it came to the females, whom the *massari* asked not to be allowed out of the ghetto. The second concern centered on the possibility that the young apprentices would be taken away from studying in the Talmud Torah. These opinions were sustained by the authority of the presiding Rabbi, Anania Coen.

The dispute − a small but eloquent example of the attitude of reciprocal and intransigent barriers between the Jewish and Christian societies as far as religion was concerned − lasted for five months. In reply to the *massari*, Samuel Castelnuovo, in the name of the initiative's other proponents, after declaring his willingness to accept their suggestion for the girls, said that thirteen was too old to learn a trade and that they had no intention of taking the young boys away from the knowledge of the *Jewish Nation's* religious traditions. This response was in vain. An anonymous report presented to the *Buongoverno* (but probably coming from the *Segreteria del Regio Diritto* [Secretary of State Law]) underlined that the *massari* continued to protest that they saw in all of that the danger of "spreading religious indifference among the Jews, of unbinding common links that today form a particular Society", and concluded that "it is impossible to persuade the religious Jews that the placement of their young children with a Christian teacher would not be a big step toward making him lose his faith". The Grand Duke, consequently and significantly, decided in favor of the *massaris*' opinion. Thus, for the moment, the initiative failed.

It was taken up again ten years later in December, 1835. After affirming that, "There has never been such disastrous time as the present for our *Nation*. Commerce which has always been her main resource no longer provides the same income even to those who engage in it most industriously", the specially appointed commission drew up a new plan which partially kept in mind the earlier attempt which had failed. The school had to be opened "in the midst of our houses or in the neighborhood", and the boys would be required to study in the *Talmud Torah* (that is, the Jewish religious school). A teacher from the *Talmud Torah* would also teach the girls to read and write. The boys would be introduced to the trades of carpenter, cabinet-maker, turner, cobbler, tailor, upholsterer, book binder, umbrella maker, goldsmith, silversmith, and the girls to those of seamstress, men's tailor, milliner, lingerie maker, embroiderer. Still awaiting solution was the problem of age, between 10 and 15 for boys and between 8 and 13 for the girls, and also that of the boys' presence in Christian stores and artisan workshops. Once again an irreconcilable difference arose between the *massari* and the initiative's supporters (gathered around the banker, Lodovico Mondolfi). And once again in July, 1836, just when the school was about to open, the whole thing ended in failure.

Although the girls' school opened in 1843, obeying the conditions set by the *massari*, the boys had to wait until 1851. Then boys between the ages of 10 and 16 years were admitted to the Institute of Arts and Trades for the Israelites of Florence (but a reform in 1859 raised the lower limit to twelve). There were one and a half hours of lessons a day, "alternating the days between religious instruction and lessons in other subjects", with the strict obligation to attend religious ceremonies and the prayers.

There were eight societies (besides the previously mentioned Tree of Life) for charitable purposes, almost all of them had long histories. The Society of the True Mercy went back to 1692. It was re-founded on December 23, 1801, with the name *Chesed Veemet* (Charity and Truth) and later reformed several times (in 1819, in 1844, and in 1849). Besides taking care of burials, which was its main purpose, it distributed coal to the poorest people to use in braziers to warm themselves in the winter. It also donated two dowries each year to girls who were about to be married. The Mortuary Society, established in 1710 and reformed in 1744, had a similar purpose. It provided the transportation of the dead from their homes to the cemetery. In addition there was the Company of the Purifiers of the Dead, founded in 1763, which obeyed the religious rule requiring the purification and preparation of the dead for burial. The society called Clothing the Naked (with the same name – *Malbish Arumin* – and with the same purposes as the one in Livorno) distributed winter clothes and bed covers to the poor. It went back to 1758. The Benefactors of the Sick had its origins in a company founded in 1671 and, starting in 1776, distributed beds and sheets to the sick. Its by-laws were reformed in 1795. The Godfathers' Society, founded in 1777, assigned a godfather, who paid for the circumcision ceremony, to poor babies. The most recent was the Society of

Personal Mercy (1822), that also took care of changing the linens on the sick people's beds.

And it didn't end there. Passerini concluded his list noting:

The Council of the Community administrated no small sum, destined to be distributed annually in charity, in dowries, in aid to pregnant women, in clothing school children, and in maintaining the nursery school. These charities came from legacies made at various times by generous benefactors, among whom Samuel Anselmo Galligo, Abigaille Gallico widow of Fano, Lea Casès, and Rachele Bonfil-Wais-Villareale are not to be forgotten

(as well as a *very generous Jew*, whose name is not mentioned, but who was said to refer to the spirit of Chiara Baraffael).

Bibliographical note

See: Luigi PASSERINI, *Storia degli Stabilimenti di beneficenza e d'istruzione elementare gratuita di Firenze* (Florence: Le Monnier, 1835), and my aforementioned essay *Breve storia degli ebrei toscani*.

A FEW WORDS ON THE CONTEMPORARY PERIOD

In the period following Italian unification and emancipation, though their specific histories differed, the problems that concerned the Florentine Jews were the same as those faced by the Italian Jews in general.

Obviously one could not expect prejudice and suspicion about the Jews to disappear from one day to the next. They were so ingrained that they occasionally appear today, even after the extreme drama of the concentration camps just a little more than fifty years ago. At the time the events seemed to have the cathartic effect of clearing up all ambiguities and doubts. But even today anti-Semitism, anti-Judaism, or anti-Hebrew feelings are sometimes expressed either implicitly or explicitly, and at times all three of these attitudes appear together.

At least during the first decades after unification, the subject of so-called Jewish "regeneration" was not the one that attracted the most attention (although the fact that a simultaneous and corresponding "regeneration" of the Christian world's attitudes towards the Jews was not as insistently called for should have caused some alarm). At first more importance was attributed to the problem of Jewish identity, which, up to that time, had been forced to remain unchangeable, fixed, and apparently timeless. That was not only because its unique cultural tradition was filled with religious rigidity, but above all, because the hostility that surrounded the Jews (both as individuals and as a group) did not permit relationships, meetings, or mixings. The Jew was obliged to remain obstinately himself. Now this same identity, so painfully acquired and so jealously kept, ran the risk of losing its precise characteristics and of becoming confused with the identity of others, up to the point of fusing with it. There were mixed marriages; conversions, sometimes dictated by convenience, but certainly not by force; access to public offices and to the political arena on the same basis as the non-Jews, as equals and without distinctions; and access to judicial positions, to university chairs and to cultural institutions. While the Jews were being accorded the rights from which they had been excluded from time immemorial and were gaining protection from offenses that had humiliated both them and those that were responsible for them, they had good reason to fear losing themselves in the process of integration and assimilation.

If we keep in mind the phenomenon of secularization that spread through both Jewish and non-Jewish society (though not at today's pace) from at least the second half of the 1800's, we can better understand the problem for those who had had religion (that particular religion) as their essential and constant reference point. Now, having become Italians, they were citizens of a secular state or one that proclaimed itself such.

The way in which Jewish financiers and businessmen increasingly and actively participated in the economic life and in the speculation that was developing at that time is proof of a hidden but ever-present danger to Jewish identity. As we have already seen, even before Italian unification, Florence had seen a consistent number of Jewish participants in its flourishing businesses, particularly in the area of acquisition and sales of real estate coming from families facing bankruptcy. Immediately following the unification, during the five-year-period when Florence was the capital of Italy, banking and real estate activities intensified, as did manufacturing, though to a lesser extent. In all this Jewish businessmen were active along with non-Jewish businessmen, and it would have been impossible to distinguish them by the business in which they were engaged, the goals that they wanted to reach, or the context in which they operated. This observation has already been made, but it is worth repeating.

The Christian banker Emanuele Fenzi, for example, behaved no differently than the Jewish banker Giacomo Servadio. The two of them were interchangeable, though the former had a fortune that went back many years, while the latter together with his brother Giuseppe seems to have been an aggressive businessman, who by means of credit operations in the building sector, according to Coppini, climbed the ladder of riches and the power that follows in its wake. Giuseppe Servadio became the substitute director of the *Banca Nazionale Toscana* in 1867 and in 1869. Giacomo founded his own bank, the *Banca di Credito Provinciale e Comunale*, based on capital coming from a predominantly Jewish bank in Livorno which had failed. He assumed the presidency in 1869. Immediately afterward he bought the Grand Hotel in Florence, participated in the company that was involved in building the Mantua-Modena railroad, associated with the *Banca Italo-Germanica*, and moved his center of operations to Rome. Beginning in 1873 after greatly enlarging his business, his credit operations, consisting mainly of advances and discounting, brought him to ruin. Together with the Passigli, therefore, the Servadio may be placed among the *nouveaux riches* with fluctuating fortunes. But next to them and like them we also meet non-Jews, like the Alinari and so many others. The families of Jewish bankers from Livorno – the Maurogordato, the Bondi, the Rodocanachi – became associated with the Fenzi, with the Bastogi and with others and shared in administrating the regional currency issuing bank along with the Florentines.

An identical phenomenon also occurred in the field of culture. The Jews of Florence began to find places in Tuscan journalism, in Italian literature, in Italian and European painting, and so on. The biography of Alessandro Franchetti (born in Livorno, but died in Florence) is no different, at least at first sight, than that of any scholar, whether Jewish or not. A bibliophile and a Dante scholar, he was one of many who, for some time, was involved in the political passion provoked by Mazzini. He was enthusiastic about Romagnosi's philosophy and was involved in historical studies concerning the Lombards. He created a *Biblioteca Dantesca* [Dante library] which he donated to the State.

Of the nine D'Ancona brothers, Sansone was a diplomat. He became the general secretary of the Tuscan Finance Ministry, was a member of Parliament from 1860 to 1865 and later a senator. Giacomo was a doctor, Vito a painter, and Cesare a professor of paleontology and botany and an eminent member of the *Accademia dei Georgofili*. Alessandro, the best known of the brothers, was a literary figure, editor of *La Nazione*, senator of the Kingdom, director of a prestigious university, the *Scuola Normale* of Pisa, as well as mayor of that city for two years.

We must also add the musician Mario Castelnuovo Tedesco,
born in Florence almost at the begining of the 1900's and later natu-
ralized American. He was the author of compositions inspired by
Shakespeare and by Hebrew sacred music, and was the winner of a
National Opera Competition in 1925. Nor can we forget that near
Florence in the *Villa I Tatti* lived and worked the great art critic and
scholar, Bernard Berenson, a Jew born in Lithuania.

Angiolo Orvieto (born in 1869 and died in 1967), who considered himself passionately Florentine, during his long life was in
close contact with literary circles which included the best known
names in Italian literature: from Pascoli to Pirandello, from Prezzo-
lini to D'Annunzio. Among other things, he founded the review *Il
Marzocco* (1896), which also had Enrico Corradini as its editor. At
least at the beginning, it was certainly at the level of similar edito-
rial initiatives that erupted on Florentine scene at the beginning of
the 1900's. In the wake of this, and almost until his death, he was
considered an essential reference point for all Italian literary culture.
For him "the conflict to resolve will essentially be to feel simultaneously and undeniably Jewish and Florentine". Among the Jewish
writers for *Il Marzocco* were great cultural personalities such as
Giulio Fano, Augusto Franchetti, Alessandro D'Ancona, Graziadio
Isaia Ascoli, etc. Their contributions were independent of their Jewish identity, upon which − in that fortunate period between the
1800's and 1900's − no doubt was cast.

Naturally, there were some who followed a different path and
tried to stay fully within Jewish tradition without excluding contact
with others and their culture. Perhaps the two most important examples we can give are Samuel Hirsch (Zvi) Margulies and Umberto (Mosè David) Cassuto.

The first, a man of great culture, particularly in Semitic languages and Biblical exegesis, came from Galicia and obtained the
job of Chief Rabbi of the Florentine community toward the end of
the 1800's, following the death of David Jakob Maroni in 1888. He
remained in Florence until his death in 1922 and was intensely active, especially after he was able to transfer the Italian rabbinical
seminary from Rome to Florence in 1899. Calling some of the most
important Hebrew scholars to collaborate with him, he made the
community of Florence the center of Jewish culture in Italy and the
starting point for youth movements advocating renewal. He founded

the *Rivista Israelitica* (1904-1915) and contributed to the foundation of the *Settimana Israelitica* (1910-1915, which later became *Israel*, 1916-1938 and 1944-1974). All these were newspapers that contributed to the birth of the *Rassegna Mensile di Israel* in 1925. Samuel Margulies adhered to Zionism and organized Theodor Herzl's visit to King Vittorio Emanuele III. Among his many disciples who became famous rabbis was Umberto Cassuto.

The references to periodicals call to mind the Jewish publishing houses of those times. Besides *Israel* which published only Jewish material and was small, there were two others: Bemporad and Olschki.

The former was founded in 1862 by Roberto Bemporad upon a preexisting publishing house which from 1840 had belonged to Alessandro and Felice Paggi, his Sienese relatives, who were originally from Pitigliano. The business reached its height under the management of Roberto's son, Enrico, who headed the company from 1893 to 1938 when the racial laws imposed a radical change. Enrico had to leave and the publishing house changed its name to "Marzocco". To tell the truth, his earlier relations with the Fascist regime had been rather stormy. Between 1924 and 1927 Enrico Bemporad seem willing to conform to the prevailing order. He approached Attilio Vallecchi and along with two other Florentine publishers – Barbèra and Salani – joined a Committee to promote the Florentine section of the Fascist Editors' Union. He was even vice-president of the Florentine Institute of Fascist Culture. Then, even before 1938, the Fascists began a vicious press campaign against the Jewish publisher, accusing him of being indirectly responsible for the death of Emilio Salgari, whose books he had printed. Salgari had committed suicide because of his economic problems.

Over and beyond these circumstances, the publishing house had accumulated many merits in the course of its history. As the heir of the Paggi brothers publication of *Pinocchio*, Bemporad gave ample room to very successful children's books. Besides the works of Salgari, he printed *Il giornalino di Gianburrasca* by Luigi Bertelli. He also published Filippo Turati's *Critica Sociale* for several years, distributed Verga's and Pirandello's writings, and audaciously began a series of both Italian and foreign works on psychology and education, etc.

Since he was against Fascism, the publisher Olschki kept his distance from it, but he was able to avoid repressive measures, at least until 1938, thanks to the type of publications he produced: works for bibliophiles, essays of great erudition or specialized culture produced by corporations, institutes, universities, etc. The publishing house had been founded in Verona in 1886 by Leo Samuele Olschki, and then moved on to Venice and finally to Florence in 1897. An important bibliophile himself, he was forced to emigrate first to France and then to Switzerland when he was past eighty because of the racial laws. The publishing house had its license as supplier to the Royal House taken away and was required to change its name. It was able to resume its activity, which continues to be intense even today, only at the end of the war. Olschki printed and continues to print well-known reviews such as *La bibliofilia*, *Archivio storico italiano*, *Rivista d'arte, Giornale dantesco*, and so on, plus numerous collections produced by academies, study centers, universities, etc. It continues to have a very ample and specialized catalogue.

Among the publishing houses, it is necessary to mention the much more recent Giuntina, born in 1980 out of a printing business which went back much earlier (1909). It has become well-known for the attention it pays to Jewish literature and essays, which make up a catalogue that has rapidly grown very rich. It includes, among other things, a series that bears the name of Schulim Vogelmann and includes works by Wiesel, Yehoshua, Mosse, Lasker-Schüler, etc.

Returning to Umberto Cassuto, who was born in Florence in 1883, we must mention, first of all, that in 1918 he published a work that is still considered a reference point and almost a model for Jewish, not only Tuscan, historiography: *Gli ebrei a Firenze nell'età del Rinascimento*. When his predecessor Margulies died, he followed him as Chief Rabbi and as director of the rabbinical seminary, but he left the job three years later to become professor of Hebrew language and literature at the University of Florence. He held the same chair in Rome starting in 1933. A great expert in Hebrew manuscripts and incunabula, he was invited to catalogue the ones in the Vatican library. As a convinced Zionist, he left Italy immediately after the Fascist regime's emanation of the racial laws and moved to *Eretz Israel* to teach at the Hebrew University.

Rabbi Margulies also had a determining influence on Alfonso Pacifici, a lawyer and a strenuous and brilliant supporter of an integral form of Judaism, in which Jewish religious and cultural traditions were to be combined with Zionism. Together with Dante Lattes – himself an essential reference point for Zionism in Italy, to which he had been introduced by Marcou Baruch – Pacifici founded important papers in Florence such as those that we have already mentioned: the weekly *Israel* and *La Rassegna Mensile di Israel*, a journal that still exists and which was destined to play a primary role in Hebrew historical studies, which had been ignored until then.

Florentine Zionism made a name for itself within the Italian Jewish milieu. It adopted one of the decisive and serious forms of Zionism, turning it into a true movement for national redemption. It was not surprising that Alfonso Pacifici moved to *Eretz Israel* as early as 1934 in order to spread his orthodox convictions by means of intense cultural and promotional activities. His was a minority position. Zionism had developed in Italy, like elsewhere, as an answer to the explosion of antisemitism that had occurred in France at the time of the *Dreyfus affair* and in Eastern Europe with a shocking series of very violent *pogroms* between the end of 19th and the beginning of the 20th century. Almost everywhere the Jews were becoming convinced that anti-semitism was a fundamental and enduring feature of the social context in which they lived, and that eliminating it would be impossible. The solution to the Jewish problem would only be possible by establishing a Jewish homeland. The process of Jewish integration was rapidly, though not totally, interrupted, and the Jews vigorously and proudly reaffirmed their identity through Zionism in a national sense (sometimes with accents as intransigent as those used by contemporary nationalisms).

But the birth and beginnings of Italian Zionism were difficult and full of contrasts. In the Jewish community of Trieste it was seen favorably; in Piedmont, instead, with suspicion. They feared that affirming its principles would cast doubt on their loyalty to the country of which they were citizens. Did the Italian Jews feel Jewish or Italian? It was an unsettling question that would be repeated in different forms and situations up to our times. Though none or very few of those who posed it questioned themselves about the prejudice implicit in asking such a thing only to the Jews. The majority of Italian Jews in that period interpreted Zionism as a movement of

solidarity toward their brothers who were once again gravely perse-
cuted in many parts of Europe. With Pacifici Florentine Zionism
was the most resolute. The loyalty of the Florentine Jews to Italy
was demonstrated by their contribution to the First World War: *280
fighters, 28 dead, 5 mutilated, 55 wounded and invalids, 17 volun-
teers, 100 decorated with medals.*

As far as their attitude toward Fascism was concerned, the Florentine Jews, like the Jews in the rest of Italy, held a great variety of
individual opinions. Some joined, some were sympathetic, some
kept their distance and some were suspicious of it. There were even
some who fought against it openly. One example that stands for all
was Carlo Rosselli, who had deep ties to Florence where he graduated from the university and founded a cultural association.

All the Jews were taken by surprise by the racial laws issued by
the regime at the end of 1938. Mixed marriages were forbidden, the
Jews were excluded from public offices and teaching, their rights to
own property and exercise business activities were severely limited,
and having *Aryan* household servants was forbidden... It certainly
was not easy to foresee that the obscure times of the Counter-reformation would return in the midst of the 20th century, thanks to a
State that the Jews had helped build. Now it declared them official
enemies of the country and of society and treated them as such.
Only the badge and ghetto were missing. And even those, not long
afterwards, would arrive under the form of concentration camps and
the badge imposed on those being deported to them. At the beginning of the Fascist racial legislation, painful internal conflicts within
the Jewish communities were not lacking, some of which developed
into serious and painful events: for instance, the print shop where
Israel was printed was attacked and destroyed by a group of Florentine Jews who supported the regime.

Even the so-called *Aryan* population was, as a whole, surprised
and disconcerted. It did not approve, but neither did it protest. And
its submissive attitude, though full of perplexity, reserve and a sense
of injustice, or at least of the senselessness of what was happening,
was not limited only to the common people. When the Jewish teachers were expelled from the university, in Florence as elsewhere,
none of their colleagues publicly expressed the indignation that they
must certainly have felt. And yet men of the stature of Federico
Cammeo, whose administrative law manuals had become classics,

of Giorgio Pacifico De Semo, a professor of commercial law, of Enrico Finzi, a professor of institutions of private law, of Renzo Ravà, an expert in labor law, of Ludovico Limentani, whose students in moral philosophy became internationally famous, of Attilio Momigliano, a very fine historian and critic of Italian literature, of Clara Capua Bergamini, a scholar in chemistry, of Enzo Bonaventura, an illustrious psychologist (who later died in Israel in 1948 during an Arab attack) were expelled from the university. Not to mention those who, like Aldo Neppi Modona, saw their careers, previously headed towards a university chair, interrupted by the Fascists' restrictions. In addition all the Jewish teachers and students were expelled from one day to the next from every type and level of school. The list would be too long to appear here.

The Florentine community, though so badly stricken, reacted like many other Italian Jewish communities with a great sense of duty and sacrifice by opening its own elementary and middle schools in 1939. The schools proved to be functional and efficient, thanks to the fact that teachers who had been expelled from the high schools and the university taught there. The community also succeeded in finding a job for many of those who had finished studying, and for a Jew finding work was quite difficult in those hard times. Even summer camps were organized for the children and assistance was given to foreign Jews who had fled to Italy. Just before the greatest tragedy, in 1943, a Delasem (Aid Delegation for Jewish Emigrants) headquarters was set up on Via de' Rustici, while the direction of the Community was taken over by Eugenio Artom, who would later be one of the most important participants in the Resistance in Florence.

During the five year period going from 1938-1943 in spite of the evidence of the iniquity, the prevalent attitude of most of the population was passivity. The "Jewish question", in all its crassness, attracted attention and stimulated feelings of solidarity only when it arrived at its extreme limit in the final years of the war. No one thought that the racial laws would be taken seriously, or applied strictly and no one saw or wished to see the grave social, moral and economic damage they caused. Thus arose the legend – that persists even today – that Mussolini made a concession to Hitler, but it would have merely been superficial and without consequences if the tragic events of 1943 had not occasioned the Wehrmacht's occupation of most of Italy.

It must be said that at the beginning not even the threat posed by that occupation was taken seriously enough by the Florentine Jews themselves, except for a few of them. Among them was Nathan Cassuto, the son of Umberto, who had just then become the Chief Rabbi. He tried as hard as possible to warn his brothers and help them find refuge, and continued to do so at the cost of his life.

The situation in Florence was made more difficult by the notable addition of foreign Jews who were obviously more difficult to hide and protect than the Italians. A committee established within the community – composed of Raffaele Cantoni, Matilde Cassin, Hans Kalberg, Wanda and Luciana Lascar, and Joseph Ziegler, in addition to Nathan Cassuto – soon realized that it would not be able to face the situation alone and turned to the Florentine church for help. Giorgio La Pira acted as a mediator with Cardinal Elia Dalla Costa who immediately agreed to help. He assigned several priests to establish contacts and to give the requested support. The most important of all was Don Leto Casini, the parish priest of Varlungo.

It was an important step and one of great significance. Those who helped the Jews knew that they were risking their own lives. More than twenty convents, both male and female, welcomed and hid many Jews, while others found hospitality in country parishes. In spite of that the Jewish community of Florence was one of the most heavily hit by searches and deportations. In the month of October about ten individual arrests took place, but the two biggest roundups took place on the 6th and the 26th of November, 1943, with the collaboration of the Fascist authorities and with the help of the thugs from the Carità gang. On the second occasion the Nazis arrested most of the members of the committee, including Don Leto Casini, and broke into three convents, capturing men, women and children. The success of the operation was due to information furnished by a spy, Felice Ischio, called Marco, who had gained the trust of the committee after being introduced by Joseph Ziegler. Don Leto Casini was freed after a little less than a month of prison, only thanks to Cardinal Dalla Costa's energetic and courageous intervention. Facing the German command, he personally assumed all the responsibility for what the priest had done.

It is impossible to indicate the exact number of the Jews thus deported. Limiting ourselves to sure information and to those who were born in the city or who officially resided there, the sum of the Jews arrested in Florence (272) or elsewhere totals 343. But this number includes only a small part of those foreign Jews that shared the same fate. It is worthwhile to cite some figures: the last arrest known to us occurred in June, 1944. Out of the total (343), twenty were children between 0 and 10 years of age. 199 people were sent to Auschwitz. Nothing is known about 122 of them. The rest were held in various death camps. There were 20 survivors, of whom 14 were arrested in Florence, but these are only the documented cases. It is necessary to observe that there were many more victims. Suffice it to say that at the end of 1943 between Florentines and foreigners, the Jews deported from Florence to the camp of Fossoli (a transit camp for Auschwitz) numbered about 500.

The last fifty years are more a chronicle than history. In 1983 the community consisted of about 1,300 people (about 1,000 today). Of those working, 42% have a commercial activity, 18% are professionals, and 23% are government employees (including teachers, who account for a large percentage). From a sociological point of view the members are mainly middle class. Ties to Jewish identity are quite varied, so much so that they are impossible to classify. They go from the strictest religious orthodoxy to cases in which every significant contact with the community had been lost. So, the recurring questions: "Who is a Jew? Who are the Jews?" come up often among them. They are questions to which it is impossible to give a single sure answer. These are also questions that anyone – and not just a Jew – finds difficult to answer with reference to the culture to which he belongs.

Bibliographical note

For the economic aspects see the works mentioned by Romano Paolo COPPINI, and also, by the same author, "Patrimoni e società anonime (1861-1894): il caso toscano", in *Annali della Fondazione Luigi Einaudi*, vol. X (1976), pp. 121-187.

For the question of the Italian-ness of the Jews: Gina FORMIGGINI, *Stella d'Italia, Stella di David. Gli ebrei dal Risorgimento alla Resistenza* (Milan: Mursia,

1970); *Gli Ebrei di Firenze per la più grande Italia*, edited by Gustavo Cassuto (Florence: Industrie Grafiche Cassuto & Amati, 1931).

For the people cited and for Jewish culture: Ugo Caffaz, "La cultura ebraica", in *Atti Vieusseux*, 3 n.d. [Firenze nella cultura italiana del Novecento]; Caterina DEL VIVO, "Angiolo Orvieto: un ebreo fiorentino", in *Bollettino a cura dell'Amicizia ebraico-cristiana di Firenze*, n.s. XXVI, 1-2; January-June 1991; Carlo A. VITERBO, "Un Maestro ancora presente," in *Rassegna Mensile di Israel*, XXVIII, 4 (April 1972) [the whole number of the review is dedicated to *Cinquant'anni dalla scomparsa di S.H. Margulies* (Fifty years from the death of Rabbi S.H. Margulies)]; Lionella VITERBO, "La nomina del rabbino Margulies. Un excursus nella Firenze di fine Ottocento", in *Rassegna Mensile di Israel*, LX (1993). Also by L. Viterbo see *Spigolando nell'archivio della Comunità ebraica di Firenze* (Florence: Giuntina, 1997).

For Zionism: Riccardo DI SEGNI, *Le origini del sionismo in Italia* (Florence: Giuntina, 1972); Francesco DEL CANUTO, *Il movimento sionistico in Italia dalle origini al 1924* (Milan: Federazione Sionistica Italiana, 1972).

For the deportations: Paola PANDOLFI, "Ebrei a Firenze nel 1943. Persecuzione e deportazione", in *Argomenti storici*, Quad. V (University of Florence, Facoltà di Magistero, 1980); Liliana PICCIOTTO FARGION, *Il libro della memoria. Gli ebrei deportati dall'Italia (1943-1945)* (Milan: Mursia, 1991), and today: *Razza e fascismo. La persecuzione contro gli ebrei in Toscana (1938-1943)*, edited by Enzo Collotti, 2 volumes (Regione Toscana-Giunta Regionale, Carocci, 1999).

For the present situation: Corinna COULMAS, "La communauté juive de Florence", in *Rassegna Mensile di Israel*, L, 1-4 (Jan.-April 1984).

DEMOGRAPHIC NOTE

To evaluate the consistence of the Jewish population from its origins to our days in Florence (as elsewhere) there are numerous and serious difficulties, some of which are insuperable.

In Tuscany, until the 1500's there was no demographic information not to speak of a census. For the whole earlier period we must proceed, therefore, by supposition and inductive reasoning. From the 16th to the 18th century there is rare and not wholly trustworthy data, gathered according to variable criteria. That means, for example, that we can find information on the whole population but not on the Jewish minority, but the opposite can also happen. Beginning at about the middle of the 18th century the Lorraine rulers in Tuscany made a more serious and organic attempt to gather information, but a real census was held only after the unification of Italy (1861), preceded in the first half of the century by a Napoleonic census in 1810 and one by the Lorraine in 1841.

For the Jews the problem is even more complex because, until the first half of the 1800's, there was no official documentation of births and deaths. The office of vital statistics until then was the parish priest who was required to register only the Christians. In the census of 1841 the job of furnishing data on the Jewish population was assigned to the rabbi. It is necessary to take into account both the Jewish resistance to being counted in a census and their notable mobility. By paradox, beginning with Italian unity when the Jews were no longer counted separately, our information is subject to other uncertainties.

For these reasons, and still others, the data in our possession is scarce and uncertain. Therefore, we warn you to use the numbers we give here, which have been taken from various sources, with great caution:

Year or period	Global population of Florence	Jews
1300	88,000	10-100
1400	80,000	10-100
1492	63,000	10-100
1570*	65,000	86
1571**	65,000	500
1622	66,000	495
1630	63,000	453
1642	70,000	549
1661	61,000	513
1674	70,000	570
1680-90	70,000	590
1730	75,000	800
1750-60	78,000	794
1784	79,000	929
1809	76,000	1,114
1841	102,000	1,543
1848	107,000	1,458
1871	188,000	2,366
1901	205,000	2,776
1938	345,000	2,326
1948	380,000	1,500
1965	445,000	1,276
1975	460,000	1,200
2000	380,000	1,000

* Before the establishment of the ghetto. ** After the establishment of the ghetto.

ESSENTIAL CHRONOLOGY

14th century – The first Jewish presence in the city.

1430 – The first Jewish settlement and possibly the first synagogue.

1437 – The birth of the Jewish Community (and Jewish loan banks).

15th and 16th centuries – Ties between the Florentine Renaissance and Jewish culture.

1527 – The end of Jewish loan banks.

1571 – The beginning of the ghetto period.

1572 – The supposed founding of the Italian rite synagogue.

1596 – The founding of the Levantine synagogue.

1636 – The House of the Catechumens founded for the conversion of the Jews.

1670-1723 – Cosimo III's government. Restrictive policy against the Jews.

1735 – The Jewish nursery school is founded.

1755 – The end of the obligation to close the ghetto gates.

1778 – Grand Duke Leopold sells the ghetto to the Jews.

1799 – Tuscany occupied by French troops. The first Jewish emancipation.

1814 – With the Restoration, the Jews return to their previous condition.

1814-1861 – The Jews participate in the *Risorgimento* (Italian unification).

1834 – The ghetto is definitively suppressed.

1848-1852 – The Statute (constitution) conceded by the King. The Jews given equal rights.

1859-1861 – The second and full emancipation of the Jews under the Kingdom of Italy.

1882 – The inauguration of the present synagogue on Via Farini.

1938-1943 – Application of the racial laws.

1943-1944 – The period of roundups and deportations by Nazis and Fascists.

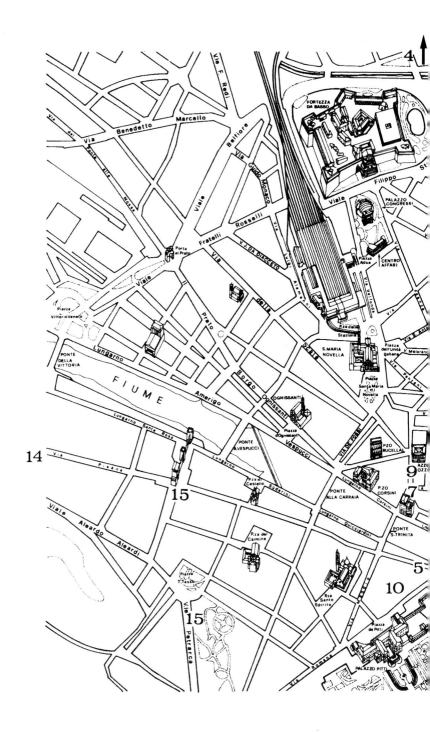

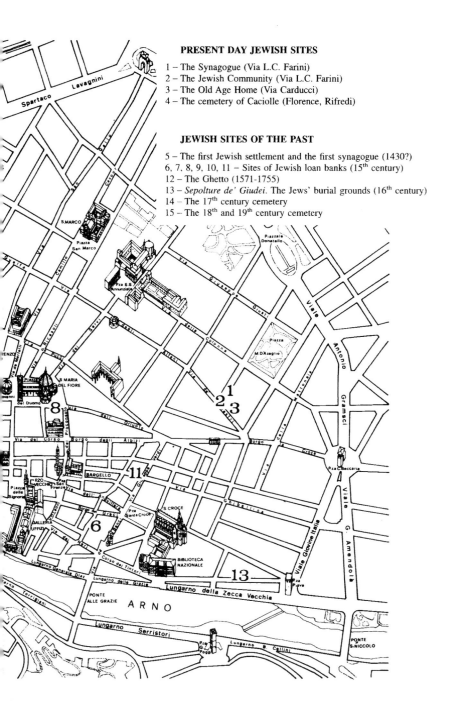

PRESENT DAY JEWISH SITES

1 – The Synagogue (Via L.C. Farini)
2 – The Jewish Community (Via L.C. Farini)
3 – The Old Age Home (Via Carducci)
4 – The cemetery of Caciolle (Florence, Rifredi)

JEWISH SITES OF THE PAST

5 – The first Jewish settlement and the first synagogue (1430?)
6, 7, 8, 9, 10, 11 – Sites of Jewish loan banks (15th century)
12 – The Ghetto (1571-1755)
13 – *Sepolture de' Giudei*. The Jews' burial grounds (16th century)
14 – The 17th century cemetery
15 – The 18th and 19th century cemetery

Finito di stampare
nella Tipografia Giuntina
Firenze, luglio 2005

COLLANA «SCHULIM VOGELMANN»